art + architecture + landscape:
The Clos Pegase Design Competition

San Francisco Museum of Modern Art

401 Van Ness Avenue
San Francisco, California 94102-4582
The Museum is supported in part by
the Institute of Museum Services, the
National Endowment for the Arts, the
California Arts Council, the San Fran-
cisco Hotel Tax Fund, and the San
Francisco Foundation.

This book is published in conjunction
with the exhibition *art + architecture
+ landscape: The Clos Pegase Design
Competition* organized by the San
Francisco Museum of Modern Art and
on view from 6 June to 25 August 1985.

Designer: Suzanne Anderson-Carey
Composition: petrographics/typeworld
Printing: GraphiCenter, Sacramento

Front cover: Courtesy of Faith
Echtermeyer
Back cover: Courtesy of Aerial
Photometrics

All biographies compiled by Heather
Hendrickson.

Photography Credits
All drawings and artworks
photographed by M. Lee Fatherree
except works by Graves/Schmidt team
photographed by Proto Acme Photo.
All models except Graves/Schmidt model
photographed by Jerry Ratto.

Library of Congress Cataloging in Publication Data
Main entry under title:

Art + architecture + landscape.

   1. Clos Pegase Winery.   2. Architecture–California–
Napa River Valley–Competitions.   3. Art–California–
Napa River Valley–Competitions.   I. Filler, Martin,
1948- . II. San Francisco Museum of Modern Art.
III. Title: Art plus architecture plus landscape.
NA6422.A78 1985   725'.4   85-8329
ISBN 0-918471-03-6

art + architecture + landscape:
The Clos Pegase Design Competition

San Francisco Museum of Modern Art

Foreword by Helene Fried

Essay by Martin Filler

Acknowledgements

I wish to thank the staff of the Museum, particularly
Donna Graves and Anne Munroe, for their continuous
assistance and support in this first exhibition organized by the Department of Architecture and Design.
Jeanne Collins and the public relations department
assisted us through both the competition and exhibition,
and Julius Wasserstein and the members of his crew
were, as always, terrific. Pam Pack's patience and attention to detail were invaluable while Heather Hendrickson,
Lydia Tanji, and my assistant Julie Ceballos provided
the support critical to any project. Suzanne Anderson-
Carey's thoughtful as well as beautiful design for the catalog was deeply appreciated. The insightful essay by
Martin Filler has colored our perception of the competition while Frank Born and Dan Friedlander's exhibition installation provides a provocative setting for the
show. A number of individuals provided invaluable assistance regarding the technical aspects of wine making,
and I would like to acknowledge Jerry Luper, Michael
Walsh, and Andre Tchelistcheff for their assistance.
The precompetition briefing was planned with the gener-
osity of Philipe Bonnafont. It is with deep appreciation
that the Museum wishes to acknowledge the jury members, Mary Livingstone Beebe, Craig Hodgetts, Hideo
Sasaki, and Robert Mondavi, for their rigorous thinking
and also Mondavi and his wife Margrit Biever for
sharing wine making in the Napa Valley with us. I am
indebted to Donald Stastny as we would not have had
a competition without his guidance and support. Most
importantly, it is with great respect for their dedication
to excellence that we thank Mr. and Mrs. Jan Shrem,
whose vision became our vision. Finally, I have enjoyed
the enthusiasm and support of Henry Hopkins who provided the leadership and courage to pursue these new
ideas. And it is with enormous respect and appreciation
that I dedicate this catalog to the artists and architects
who joined us in the adventure to design Clos Pegase.

H.F.

Contents

Foreword

It began simply enough: a conversation between Henry T. Hopkins, Director of the San Francisco Museum of Modern Art, and Jan Shrem, businessman and collector, in the early spring of 1984. Having recently moved from Paris, Shrem talked about his reasons for coming to California–to build a winery in the Napa Valley, to produce a great wine, to create a wonderful environment in which to live and work.

Hopkins, who announced the establishment of a Department of Architecture and Design at the Museum in the fall of 1983, asked about the selection of an architect for this ambitious endeavor. Shrem suggested the idea of a competition that would seek out an architect to create an "epoch making design." Within weeks, the Museum began to investigate the possibility of sponsoring an innovative competition to design Clos Pegase. An open, two-tiered design competition was announced, one which would emphasize the collaboration between architects and artists to design a new environment–a combination of art and wine making. In the process, the Museum hoped to expand the boundaries of both professions and set a new standard for the inventive integration of fine art with a commercial project.

After a long telephone call late on a Friday afternoon and a hasty meeting at the Portland, Oregon, airport, Donald Stastny agreed to serve as the professional advisor. Stastny, an architect active in the Northwest, had recently served as the advisor to the Beverly Hills Civic Center Competition and was certain he wasn't going to do another. However, intrigued by the scope of the project and appreciating the need to obtain good professional advice, he agreed. The Museum was ready to proceed.

It was a fast track. The announcement of the competition was made in May 1984. The projected schedule called for submissions to be received by 15 June, with interviews of the ten semifinalists thirteen days later. The five finalist teams assembled in the Napa Valley on 9 July, a mere seven days following their selection.

On the day of the deadline the reception area of the Museum was crowded with architects, artists, and delivery services submitting the required material–five examples of projects by each architect and artist. Presentation is always important, and the proposals ranged from the most beautifully designed portfolios with handmade paper and custom portfolio cases, to the simplest folder with black-and-white duplications of photographs. Impressed, initially by the sheer outpouring of material, and then later, following the review of the material, by the awesome talent these presentations represented, the selection committee made its decision.

The telephone calls to the ten semifinalists were full of the promise of the competition. Developed randomly, the schedule for their fifty-minute interviews began with Batey/Mack/Saari and ended thirty hours later with Mangurian/Turrell. Several of the teams had worked together prior to the competition; some were made up of friends, others had sought one another out in order to enter the competition. Always interesting, often provocative, and occasionally awkward, the interviews reflected the architects' and artists' struggle to find ways in which to express their shared visions.

The final selections made, the five architect/artist teams and the jury headed for the Napa Valley where they took over the small St. Helena Hotel. The day of the precompetition briefing dawned hot and still as we gathered at the gallery above La Belle Heléne restaurant. A quiet tension filled the room as the teams listened intently to Stastny present the design program. The long summer day was spent on technical presentations, tours of the Vichon and Trefethen wineries, and a late afternoon visit to the knoll.

The teams began to design. The very nature of a competition demands rigorous activity–a stretching of one's professional and personal skills. As teams and individuals, these men and women pushed themselves to the limit. As I visited them by telephone or in person, I was struck by their sense of total commitment–artists and architects wrestling with ideas, sometimes with one another.

Young students from Cal crowded into Stanley Saitowitz's Russian Hill apartment/office, with Saitowitz, Toby Levy, Pat O'Brien, and Elyn Zimmerman all seeming to design and draw simultaneously, the scent of take-out Chinese food always in the air as the twenty-four hour sessions wore on.

Moving the project temporarily from their picturesque Vandewater alley office to a light-filled space tucked under a roof and reached at the end of a myriad of hallways, Batey & Mack experimented with watercolor rather than their usual airbrush presentation drawings. Maya Lin, in San Francisco for the summer, hand cut layers of cork to build the form of their model that would be covered by thin layers of silvery blue plaster. It was Peter Saari, working in New Jersey on his gesso and plaster wall piece, who would eventually determine the colors and surfaces of the buildings–reflecting an intuitive understanding of the colors and textures of the region.

Dan Solomon and his team–professional, committed, almost driven–travelled the farthest to work with Ricardo Bofill and the Taller de Arquitectura in Paris. Visiting the studio in San Francisco, one could see their commitment: Bobbie Stauffacher Solomon creating the most beautiful of drawings with hundreds of colored pencil dots; Patrick Dillon, bent over a drawing table, producing the site plan with soft graphite; and two young Dutch architects, who had arrived earlier in the summer, building the intricately detailed red-colored model with its twisted wire trees and steel wool bushes. To the north in Portland, Oregon, Ed Carpenter completed his drawing of the leaded-glass skylight and prepared to drive south, securing it to the top of his car like a canoe.

Of equal professional experience and maturity, Jim Turrell and Robert Mangurian began their ongoing dialogue at Mangurian's Venice, California studio which resulted in an extraordinary collaboration. Ajax, a talented young designer from San Francisco, joined the team to prepare what would prove to be a history-making effort. Their beach-front, garagelike studio was filled with working models, paper samples, furniture designs, walls dripping with Italian posters, and racks of small plaster sheets drying in preparation for their transformation into the walled structures atop the knoll of the "seven mysteries." Imaginative, risk-taking, and courageous, this collaboration set a new standard for architects and artists working together.

Michael Graves and Ted Schmidt had worked together previously and shared a similar esthetic. They were supported by the brilliant team from the Graves office led by Juliet Richardson-Smith and Terry Smith. The Princeton summer demanded the best of a group known to be among the best and ended with a last-minute dash to meet the Pacific daylight time deadline, shipping West a design that would be under construction a year later. As the model and drawings were unpacked, it was clear that there had been no holding back.

For the Museum, the significance of the Clos Pegase Design Competition rested with the investigation of the issues of collaboration between artist and architect and the challenge presented by the integration of art with the business of wine making. We dared to pose the question; at best, our inquiry was imperfect. And yet it is our hope that the relationships developed and the experiences felt added to the vocabulary of both professions.

Helene Fried
San Francisco
April 1985

8

Five Designs in Search of a Patron:
On a Hilltop in Arcadia
by Martin Filler

The most highly publicized architectural commission awarded in the United States during 1984 was that for the new J. Paul Getty Fine Arts Center in Los Angeles. It has been heralded as the prize American project of the eighties. But at virtually the same time as the final phases of the selection process for the Getty Center were occurring, some five hundred miles to the north another contest was taking place, one that may eventually be considered of even greater importance in exploring some of the most pertinent concerns and stylistic trends in architecture in this decade–the Clos Pegase Design Competition, sponsored by the San Francisco Museum of Modern Art.

The two efforts could scarcely have been more different, either in terms of each client's brief or of the method each adopted to satisfy it. The Getty commission was not awarded on the basis of proposed schemes, but rather on a general impression the selection committee gathered from the work to date of three finalists selected after a worldwide search. That institution sought a designer of established international stature, as evidenced by their penultimate choice of Fumihiko Maki of Japan, Richard Meier of the United States, and James Stirling of Great Britain, among whom Meier emerged triumphant. On the other hand, Jan Shrem, the patron of the proposed Clos Pegase winery, was less concerned about the status of his architect (in fact three of the five finalists in his competition have built very little indeed). It was more important to Shrem that the winning design fill the complex and highly specific set of requirements he had in mind when he first conceived his plan to establish a home and a winemaking business in the Napa Valley.

Close to one hundred firms responded to the call for proposals for the Clos Pegase commission. A screening procedure narrowed the search to ten teams who were then interviewed, after which five finalists were chosen. It was wisely decided that in the third and final phase of the selection procedure actual designs would be submitted, fully documented in plans, presentation drawings, and models. Thus there would be less likelihood of comparing apples and oranges: with the large number of specific features desired by the client, there could be little leeway for the broad divergences that can occur in competitions in which the patron's charge to the architects is less precise.

One of the more unusual aspects of the Clos Pegase brief was the stipulation that each architect work in concert with an artist. Over the last ten years, the interaction between architecture and art has been a widely discussed issue in both professions–a factor further adding to the importance of this competition. Efforts to promote greater cooperation between artists and architects have not always been conspicuous successes. The most visible recent example was in 1981 when *Collaboration* was organized as a travelling exhibition by the Architectural League of New York to celebrate the centennial of that organization, chartered to encourage a closer integration of architecture, painting, and sculpture. With very few exceptions, the results of the show's eleven pairings were disappointing. But the impulse to stimulate a working relationship of that sort was clearly a correct one, as borne out three years later by the impressive roster of artists who were willing to join with architects in the Clos Pegase competition. Avant-garde architects who submitted qualifications but were not included in the final five teams include Ace Architects, Peter Eisenman, Frederick Fisher, Jennings & Stout, Herb Greene, Donlyn Lyndon and Marvin Buchanan, Charles Moore, Rob Quigley and Tom Grondona, Thomas Gordon Smith, William Turnbull, Jr., and Tod Williams. Among the well-established figures on the contemporary art scene who did not make it to the finals were Vito Acconci, Lita Albuquerque, Larry Bell, Laddie John Dill, Mark di Suvero, Mary Miss, Robert Morris, Ed Moses, Beverly Pepper, Arnaldo Pomodoro, and

Richard Serra. One can no longer claim that the fear of an architect's domination in such collaborations acted as a deterrent, for the artists attracted to the Clos Pegase competition were a remarkable group, both in the quality of their work and the strength of their interest.

The interaction of art and architecture was but one part of the jury's considerations in deciding the winner of the competition. As admirable as that aspect was, it was obviously not the uppermost criterion in the minds of the jury, which necessarily concerned itself primarily with the practical operations of both the winery and the residence. In this case, "practical" does not mean solely functional, for the owner wanted a design that would fulfill certain symbolic and imagistic roles that are less subject to dispassionate analysis than, say, the specifics of circulation or the correct order of wine production.

Even though the extensive givens presented to the five finalists understandably produced certain similarities among the proposals, the exceptionally diverse results make a project-by-project discussion of each the only satisfactory way to evaluate their relative strengths and weaknesses. It must be said at this point that the overall standard of the five final submissions was exceptionally high, an indication of the abilities of these teams in particular. There is no doubt that some of the prospective entrants would have performed no less interestingly had they been asked to participate in this last round, but it would be hard to imagine a more satisfying range of approaches than that presented here.

Fearful Symmetry: Andrew Batey and Mark Mack with Peter Saari

As architects who know the Napa Valley well – Batey lives there and Batey & Mack have executed several buildings there – it might have been expected that they would have devised a design that responded to their intimate understanding of the place and its architecture. Surprisingly, their scheme was one of the most rigid and formal, and their model by far the most abstract and least concerned with establishing some sense of context. The most prominent element of the Batey/Mack/Saari scheme is a wood-frame tower that creates, more emphatically than any other entry, the visible presence from the nearby highway that the competition program called for. Though certainly prominent, the tower is without any local precedent; as is often the case with such impositions on a landscape (one thinks of the Eiffel Tower), it can come to pass that the object in due course provides the identification for the place, rather than vice versa.

At the base of the hill, the Batey/Mack/Saari scheme proposes two long, low structures to house the winery. Parallel to one another, they are linked by a walkway that connects two cylindrical forms – one negative (with a peripheral ramp that is reminiscent of James Stirling and Michael Wilford's sculpture court at the Neue Staatsgalerie in Stuttgart) and the other positive, its roof elevated above the level of the rest of the winery. Painted sculptures by Saari, like weathered fragments of ancient architecture, would have helped to convey the grandeur the architects were seeking.

The residence projected by the team displays their interest in symmetry, though the rather severe forms of the two flanking wings do not have the same relaxed air of Batey & Mack's more successful residential designs in surrounding communities. Perhaps the most pleasant and promising component of the Batey/Mack/Saari design is the scattering of follies that would have dotted the hillside, offering surprising and delightful architectural incidents that seem conspicuously lacking in the scheme at large. But even these are not conveyed with sufficient persuasiveness by the architects' model,

10

which in several respects seems the least satisfactory of the five submitted. Devoid of any representational reference to the thick vegetation that covers the site, the model is covered in a bluish-white plaster wash that makes it seem as though the denuded hilltop has been hit by an ice storm. Regrettably, the entrants' renderings of their scheme are no more skillfully executed. As a result, such merits as the design has can easily fall on blind eyes.

To be sure, there is no real correlation between an alluring presentation technique and the inherent quality of an architectural design. But, especially within the context of a design competition, such gestures are necessary and legitimate parts of the architectural process. One likely explanation for the weakness of this entry could be attributed to the then-impending split in Batey & Mack's partnership. But given the uncommonly high standard of their past work, it is to be expected that future projects in this part of the world will bring forth the kind of response that their record to date promises.

Planetary Positioning:
Robert Mangurian with James Turrell

Among the five Clos Pegase finalists, none better displays how mutually inspiring an artist/architect collaboration can be when both are operating on the same wavelength as does the Mangurian/Turrell proposal. Emphatically axial, with a strong processional route linking house and winery, this design is formal in the best sense of the word. As opposed to three of the four other entries, this one does not use the contribution of the artist as an appliqué to the architectural conception, but rather it enters into an inseparable interrelationship with it.

Turrell's proposals—which include the use of framing elements around the perimeter of the courtyard roofs in both house and winery to illusionistically frame and "pull in" the sky, as well as tunnels burrowed into the hillside to align with the rays of the sun at the summer solstice—are totally in keeping with his predominant interest in light and perceptions of space. Yet they also complement Mangurian's forms with an almost architectonic force. The architect's strongly defined massing, both in the foursquare volumes of the winery and the more sculpturally detailed residence atop the hill, are beautifully augmented by colors that range from the bold to the delicate (several of which relate to plants and minerals native to the Napa Valley).

The architect's model, though again without any indication of trees and other hillside vegetation, is an object of such exquisite craftsmanship that one's attention is not detrimentally distracted as it is in the Batey/Mack/Saari model. Painstakingly cast from plaster, each minute element in the Mangurian/Turrell scheme has a crispness and clarity that emphasizes the balance that prevails in this design between power and precision. In certain respects, there are vague resemblances to the work of Michael Graves in general, and even some similarities to his winning scheme in the Clos Pegase competition in particular. Such motifs as the small, peak-roofed light monitors over the front portion of the winery structure recall Graves's San Juan Capistrano Library, for example, while the vernacular farm buildings of Tuscany obviously served as the common source of inspiration for both Mangurian and Graves.

The Mangurian/Turrell design is, however, at once more aggressively stylish and less sweetly sentimental than the Graves/Schmidt entry. Its classicizing elements, less literally employed than in the Graves/Schmidt design, have a certain New Wave twist that gives them a feeling of contemporary authenticity rather than historical recall. It is no wonder that the jury, which came closer to premiating this entry than it did any other aside from the winner, saw fit to single it out for special mention.

Circular Reasoning: Stanley Saitowitz, Toby Levy, and Pat O'Brien with Elyn Zimmerman

The one entry to make extensive use of the circle and segments of it, this scheme also addresses more directly than the other four finalists the cone-shaped hill that dominates the site. Stanley Saitowitz, whose architectural vocabulary is among the most personally idiosyncratic of his generation, took the circle as the basic plan generator of the hilltop residence, deploying the living areas in two wedge-shaped wings with the central portion of the inscribed circle "cut out" to form a piazza with views across the valley. The most extensive landscape alterations proposed by any of the teams called for clearing a wedge-shaped portion of the hillside facing the winery to the south, a demarcation emphasized by a row of poplar trees on each side. Sculptor Elyn Zimmerman's subtle contributions reiterated the circle theme: four arc-shaped fountains, ranged around the hillside like segments of a broken but continuous ring, would have caught the light as it shone off the shallow cascades and would have given the Clos Pegase site the kind of dramatic visibility called for in the program.

The winery building proper, more overtly industrial-appearing than those in the other proposals, was unusually well thought out, no doubt reflecting Saitowitz's previous experience with the building type (his design for the Quady Winery in Madera, California, is now nearing completion). Unlike most of the other schemes, there is little attempt to link the house and the winery either compositionally, physically, or symbolically in an architectural sense, but rather the beautifully worked landscape elements provide the strongest connection. Whether or not that would have

suffiiced to give the complex a convincing unity in physical reality will of course never be known, but it seems clear that given the unequally distributed emphases placed on "art + architecture + landscape" in each design, the landscape in the Saitowitz/Levy/O'Brien/Zimmerman team entry was the most imaginatively considered. However, the model conveys that with merely a mild degree of success. Although not as forbiddingly bare as the Batey/Mack/Saari and Mangurian/Turrell presentations, it does not give as good an idea as the Graves/Schmidt and Solomon/Bofill/Dillon/Stauffacher Solomon/Carpenter team models do of actual site conditions. Far more evocative are the superb airbrush renderings that Saitowitz prepared, which offer, if not precisely a realistic depiction of the Napa Valley terrain, then at least a very good feeling of how these buildings would relate to their surroundings.

This was the one scheme to employ an architectural vocabulary that was not in some way attempting a reference to either historical or regional precedents. Neither modernist nor high-tech, this design, especially when viewed alongside the four other finalists, does seem to be both more "modern" and more "technological" than any of the others–an intriguing indication of the extent to which the language of Post-Modernism has in recent years come to define the norm in avant-garde architectural expression.

The Red Fort: Dan Solomon, Ricardo Bofill and Patrick Dillon, Barbara Stauffacher Solomon with Ed Carpenter

There is something deeply compelling about this scheme, which seems reminiscent of the dense and defensive architecture of ancient Assyria. The impression is conveyed very strongly by the model, which in some respects is the most beautiful of the five as an object: its rich, reddish-brown coloration is indeed similar to the soil in parts of the Napa Valley, but here everything—architecture, vineyards, and trees—has been given that same ruddy hue. Along with the Graves/Schmidt model, this one conveys the best impression of what the wooded hill of the site actually looks like. If the way the architecture and landscape coexist is of any importance in a commission—and here it is central—then it is essential that some attempt be made to suggest how the two will interact in reality.

The impression of Near Eastern precedent is particularly strong in the winery portion of this entry. With walls rising sheer above an aeration pond—giving it the appearance of a moat—files of palm trees nearby, and a roof ranged with grapevines in a configuration reminiscent of what the Hanging Gardens of Babylon are believed to have looked like, this portion of the design has a solidity and archaic power oddly lacking in the other entries that take historical forms as a departure point.

The hilltop residence is "linked" to the winery by a narrow water channel that runs down to the level of the valley floor through a cleared portion of the hillside. Like the winery (and unlike the other house designs in the competition), the residence has a densely compacted, almost fortresslike feeling. Its strongly rooted base, severe symmetry, and small window openings, recalling the fenestration of both Spanish Colonial and Art Deco architecture, impart an aura of recession and removal from the landscape.

A leaded-glass window—a spine bisecting the winery by Portland, Oregon, artist Ed Carpenter—is more in the spirit of art-as-appliqué (shared in the Graves/Schmidt and Batey/Mack/Saari schemes) rather than art-as-integral-component (as in the Saitowitz/Levy/O'Brien/Zimmerman and Mangurian/Turrell proposals). Actually, the ravishing graphic interpretation ("rendering" would be incorrectly representational) of this

design by Barbara Stauffacher Solomon offers even better proof of the reciprocal inspiration that art and architecture can provide one another. Although immeasurably different in esthetic approach from the model, this drawing manages to capture the essential character of the scheme without attempting to imitate what is shown in the model.

The participation of Ricardo Bofill—the only non-American involved in any of the design teams—was limited, although Patrick Dillon, a member of Bofill's Taller de Arquitectura, was an active participant in the team. A number of the ideas of the Spanish architect were incorporated into the design as presented, accounting for the scheme's divergence from the Bay Area vernacular style (lately with more historicizing references) that has typified the work of the Solomon office, and movement toward a more self-consciously allusive approach speaking of other times and other places.

The Spirit of the Places:
Michael Graves with Edward Schmidt

The architecture of Michael Graves for some time now has drawn on the rustic, agrarian architecture of Northern Italy as a major source of formal inspiration, but only with occasional success. While the appropriateness of his library for San Juan Capistrano—that Williamsburg of Spanish Colonial architecture—cannot be contested, the application of that same stylistic mode to an environmental study center on the New Jersey side of New York harbor is highly debatable. But at last Graves has an opportunity to put his deeply felt beliefs about the need for a return to a more representational architecture into practice with a commission that offers very promising potential to prove his argument.

It is easy for both professionals and laymen to understand why the Graves/Schmidt scheme won. Graves, with considerable experience in entering, and more importantly, winning architectural design competitions, is well aware that, save for juries made up entirely of his coprofessionals, it is necessary for those who want to win to make their presentations as beautiful and realistic as possible. That he has done here. The surprisingly schematic models offered by some of the other entrants give the impression, whether based in fact or not, of incompletely developed ideas. That could never be said of the Graves/Schmidt scheme, which is displayed with a conceptual thoroughness that goes beyond its carefully executed details.

The familiar villagelike clusters of buildings that Graves has produced again and again in his recent large-scale designs are present here again, but with a practical difference: they offer the client the possibility of realizing the project in gradual increments if so 14 desired, a distinct possibility once the client faces the practical realities of bringing his extraordinary ambitious dream to reality in one fell swoop. Furthermore, the approach (as opposed, say, to the monolithic massing of the Batey/Mack/Saari or Solomon/Bofill/Dillon/ Stauffacher Solomon/Carpenter schemes) affords the compositional diminution of what might be seen locally as architecture too overbearing for its setting. Though indeed dramatic, the knoll that crowns the Clos Pegase site is by no means the largest in the vicinity, and its size suggests that a domestic scale is the correct one to pursue there.

Functionally, the Graves/Schmidt scheme was decreed to be the best by those with a knowledge of the wine-making business. That factor, combined with the scheme's alluring esthetic, its gestures to tradition and region, and a highly romantic conception of its function, made it the most logical choice for the jury. Edward Schmidt's murals, portraying the cycle of wine making, are conceived in representational style that is in spirit-ual accord with Graves's beliefs about architecture. It is both interesting and ironic that the owner, whose art collection has centered on the work of the Surrealists, will be sponsoring art of such a neo-realist sort. But it must also be said that Graves's architecture, which does not easily admit intervention of things not prescribed for it by its designer, could not easily assimilate anything but a work chosen by this most comprehensive of estheticians.

The ironies do not end there. In his original brief, the client expressed his desire for architecture that took its cues from Japanese design, typified by structures that fit into the landscape rather than dominating it, blurring the hard demarcation between indoor and outdoor, and flexible in their internal organization. As it turns out, the premiated design is the very opposite of what the client at first had in mind (although it should be added that none of the other four teams followed that aspect of his directions very closely either).

But the fact that the client and the jury felt this to be the plan most likely to fulfill his larger goals for Clos Pegase is an interesting example of how persuasive design can be in taking a patron from one set of assumptions and carefully moving him to a very different point on the compass of taste. Michael Graves is not just a very accomplished architect: he is a strong and extremely influential teacher, and there is a pronounced streak of the didactic in his designs, which encourage us to experience things in just the way he wants us to, rather than being subject to the open-ended experience of most modernist architecture. Graves has points to make, and so does Jan Shrem. His conception of Clos Pegase as a place for enlightenment and inspiration has found a very clear echo in his architect's interpretation, and it makes the outcome of the competition seem fitting in a way one might not have considered if Graves were commissioned before this lengthy competition procedure unfolded itself.

The Clos Pegase story and its denouement bring to mind another California dream of almost seventy years earlier. The complex that Frank Lloyd Wright designed atop Olive Hill in Los Angeles for Aline Barnsdall between 1916 and 1920–including a house, studios, theatrical spaces, and a kindergarten, among other components–had the very same air of an Arcadian idyll that transfuses the Graves design. The particularly Californian mixture of optimism and opportunity, education and entertainment, earnestness and escapism that animated the only partially realized Barnsdall project finds a touching contemporary counterpart in the Clos Pegase competition. Although the participation of several of the most talented young architects active in America today gives this effort a special importance in gauging the state of the art form as of 1984, the real value of what has been done and still remains to be accomplished is that the spirit of idealism, which has not been in conspicuous oversupply in architecture in recent years, appears to be alive and well.

In his letter to the professional community announcing this competition, the San Francisco Museum of Modern Art's Director, Henry T. Hopkins, wrote that "by exploring the collaboration between artist and architect we would expand the boundaries of our professions and further enhance the advancement of architecture and design." That is a very tall order, to be sure, but there can be little doubt that it has been furthered here. But more importantly, in a world of increasingly narrowing artistic and architectural horizons it demonstrates that there are great rewards indeed to be won by widening our field of vision.

Martin Filler is an architecture and design critic. Formerly editor of Architectural Record Books at McGraw-Hill Publications, since 1979 he has been editor of *House & Garden* magazine. Along with architectural historian Rosemarie Haag Bletter, he wrote the award-winning 1983 film, *Beyond Utopia: Changing Attitudes in American Architecture*, directed by Michael Blackwood. He is one of the guest curators for the Whitney Museum of American Art's 1985 exhibition *High Styles: Twentieth-Century American Design* in New York.

15

The Jurors

Mary Livingstone Beebe

The vision and commitment of a private patron undertaking this adventure with the support of the San Francisco Museum of Modern Art is inspiring. I am excited by the promise of this competition, and of a vital and fruitful collaboration in which artists and architects assume new roles. This project is especially meaningful for me because, like so many in our field, I am interested in finding new ways for artists to have a significant impact on our structures and environments.

Mary Livingstone Beebe is the Director of the Stuart Collection at the University of California, San Diego, a program designed to place works by contemporary American and European artists on the 1200-acre campus in La Jolla. Since the project's inception in 1981, Beebe has commissioned site-specific works by Robert Irwin and Richard Fleischner. Beebe served as Executive Director of the Portland Center for the Visual Arts, Oregon, from 1973 to 1981. Educated at Bryn Mawr College, Pennsylvania (B.A., 1962), and the Sorbonne, L'École du Louvre, Paris, Beebe was awarded a National Endowment for the Arts fellowship in 1979. She has served on the boards of the Art Museum Association of America from 1978 to 1983 and the Henry Gallery, University of Washington, Seattle, from 1977 to 1980. Recognized for her commitment to art in public places, Beebe is currently a member of arts advisory committees to the Port of San Diego and the Centre City Development Corporation, San Diego.

Craig Hodgetts

The brief was daring, a challenge to professional guidelines which proposed collaboration not simply between architect and client, but between architect and artist, client and museum. The models and drawings evidence a commitment and intelligence all too rare in architectural circles, and illuminate a particularly elusive issue: how to give meaning, as well as delight, to the shape of our environment.

Craig Hodgetts is an architect highly regarded for his innovative industrial, film, and theatrical designs. He was educated at General Motors Institute, Flint, Michigan (1956-58); Oberlin College, Ohio (B.A., 1960); San Francisco State University (M.A. Playwriting, 1962); University of California, Berkeley (1963-65); and Yale University, New Haven, Connecticut (M. Arch., 1968). From 1969 to 1980, Hodgetts was a principal of S T U D I O W O R K S, Venice, California, and New York, which he cofounded. He is recognized as an educator and was a founding dean of the California Institute of the Arts, Valencia, in 1969. Since 1982 he has been a principal designer of Hodgetts and Fung, Los Angeles, which received a 1985 *Progressive Architecture* award for The Cookie Express store design. He recently collaborated on theatrical designs with the Mark Taper Forum, Los Angeles, and with the Museum of Contemporary Art, Los Angeles, on *Carplays* (1984). He is currently working with Charles Kober and Associates, Los Angeles, on a competition for the 1988 Olympic Village in Seoul, Korea.

Henry T. Hopkins

As Director of the San Francisco Museum of Modern Art, I am particularly pleased that we could serve as matchmakers between an inspired patron and a group of excellent architects and artists. This promises to be a landmark project in which traditional roles are intentionally blurred to allow room for integrated creativity.

Since 1974, Director Henry T. Hopkins has organized many landmark exhibitions including *Clyfford Still*, 1976; *Painting and Sculpture in California: The Modern Era*, 1976, with Walter Hopps; *Expressionism: A German Intuition, 1905-1920*, 1981, with Thomas Messer of The Solomon R. Guggenheim Museum, New York, and Dr. Paul Vogt of the Museum Folkwang in Essen, West Germany; and *The Human Condition: San Francisco Museum of Modern Art Biennial III*, 1984. In 1983, Hopkins initiated the development of an Architecture and Design Department at the Museum. He was the Director of the Fort Worth Art Museum from 1968 until 1973 and served on the staff of the Los Angeles County Museum of Art from 1961 to 1968. He was educated at the College of Idaho, Nampa (1946-49); School of The Art Institute of Chicago (B.A.E., 1952, M.A.E., 1955); and University of California, Los Angeles (1957-60). Hopkins has served on several National Endowment for the Arts panels and was appointed Chairman of the Museum Policy Panel of the National Endowment for the Arts in 1981, 1982, and 1983. He is currently serving as President of the Association of Art Museum Directors.

Robert Mondavi

I am tremendously excited and inspired by this example of integrating some of the finest artistic talent available with an effective, producing winery. I believe this project will set the tone and pace for new winery developments to come.

Robert Mondavi is a prominent figure in the international wine community. Founder of the Robert Mondavi Winery (1966) in Oakville, California, Mondavi entered the wine business after graduating from Stanford University, California, in 1936. He worked with his father at the Sunnyhill Winery (now the Sunny St. Helena Winery) and the Charles Krug Winery, both in St. Helena, California. Mondavi became recognized as one of the first local vintners to utilize technical developments to improve the wine-making process. By cold fermenting wines to retain fruitiness, he created the Chenin Blanc and Fume Blanc wines. He has recently collaborated with Baron Philippe de Rothschild in the production of *Opus One*, a premium cabernet-style wine which combines French vinification techniques with American technical expertise. Mondavi is active in numerous projects which sponsor the promotion of fine food and wine, most notably the Great Chefs of France and America Cooking Schools operated by the Robert Mondavi Winery, Oakville, California, which feature internationally known culinary figures. He serves as Director of the American Institute of Wine and Food and was chosen as Wine Maker of the Year in 1982 by the American Wine Society.

Hideo Sasaki

The fact that this was a real project with a real client whose enthusiasm for the arts brought this competition into being made this a fascinating project to be involved with. The program was interesting because the artist/architect teams had to balance practical problems of the production and marketing of wine with the personal requirements of the client, while maintaining the spirit of idealism and experimentation which motivated their collaboration. People can judge the success of each balance for themselves.

Hideo Sasaki is an internationally renowned pioneer in landscape architecture, recognized for his promotion of design excellence and scholarship. He is the founder of Sasaki Associates, Watertown, Massachusetts, and Sasaki Walker Associates (now SWA Group), San Francisco. Sasaki taught at Harvard University, Cambridge, Massachusetts, from 1950 to 1970, where he served as Chairman of the Department of Landscape Architecture from 1958 to 1968. He was educated at Reedley College, California (A.A., 1939); University of Illinois at Urbana-Champaign (B.F.A. in Landscape Architecture, 1946); and Harvard University, Cambridge, Massachusetts (M.F.A. in Landscape Architecture, 1948). He served on the United States Commission of Fine Arts from 1962 to 1972 and was a juror for the Vietnam Memorial Competition, Washington, D.C. (1981), and the Times Square Competition, New York (1984). Sasaki currently serves as a consultant to various institutions and agencies.

Donald J. Stastny

Professional Advisor

A man with a dream. An institution with a mission. An agreement to build a commercial and residential complex that is art in itself.
These were the opportunities that led to this exploration into collaboration. It was difficult and trying for everyone concerned, but the magic that evolved through the process will affect our lives for years to come. As one juror said "...The echos of this design competition will be heard far beyond this day."

Principal of Stastny Architects P.C., Portland, Oregon, since 1975, Donald Stastny is a founder of the Oregon School of Design, Portland. Stastny has worked with major firms including Kevin Roche John Dinkeloo Associates, Hamden, Connecticut. Recent projects of Stastny Architects P.C. include the Alaska Courts Complex, Anchorage (1985), with McCool-McDonald of Alaska, Anchorage, and the renovation of the historic Princeton Building, Portland, Oregon (1985). Stastny received his B.S. in Business Administration from Oregon State University, Corvalis, in 1965; his B. Arch. from the University of Washington, Seattle, in 1967; and his M. Arch. and Master of City Planning from the University of Pennsylvania, Philadelphia, in 1969. In 1984, Stastny was appointed Chairman of the Central City Committee Plan for Portland, Oregon, and is the National Endowment for the Arts Regional Design Arts Coordinator. He served as professional advisor to both the Portland Pioneer Courthouse Square, Oregon (1980), and the Beverly Hills Civic Center, California (1982), competitions.

The Report of the Jury

Odilon Redon, *Pegasus*, ca. 1900, gouache on paper, 9¹/₁₆ x 12¹⁵/₁₆″ (23 x 32.8) (sight), Mr. and Mrs. Jan Shrem

View from the knoll

The jury has had the distinct privilege of being the first to view the efforts of five talented and dedicated teams. The owner could build any one of the five design concepts and have an epoch-making winery, sculpture garden, and residence unmatched in the complex relationship of use, site, ambience, and spirit.

The theme of this competition was collaboration—easy to request, difficult to achieve. True collaboration cannot always be clearly perceived or delineated. The jury used a simple test in its evaluation: Was the presented design concept of greater content than one would expect from either the individual architect or the artist? In most cases it was. There was evidence of concepts that resulted from artists leading, concepts attributed to architects leading, and particular concepts that could only have come from the spiritual joining of kindred talents.

Further evaluation was based on the following considerations: architecture in relation to time and place; site planning and circulation; private vs. public spaces; integration of art and the treatment of architecture as art; technical requirements of the winery; the potential of phasing construction; the sense of place that resulted from the distribution of functions over the site; and, finally, the "business" of making and selling wine.

While each proposal was given the intense and immediate attention it deserved, the jury also had a long-range vision regarding the evaluation of these works. To combine the efforts of architects and artists in a task of uncommon vision, to advocate a dedication to excellence, to offer a contribution to the quality of life in the West–the jury wishes to commend the architects and artists who participated in this competition, the San Francisco Museum of Modern Art, and the owners, Mr. and Mrs. Jan Shrem. As one juror said, "We will hear the echoes of this competition for years to come."

Jury Decision

The jury, by unanimous acclamation, found two design concepts to be of the highest excellence. These two–the Graves/Schmidt proposal and the Mangurian/Turrell proposal–represent a polarity in the interpretation of the architectural design program presented to the teams. Each demonstrates individual and innovative approaches that reach far beyond the commonplace. The jury by majority vote presented the Award of the Jury to the Graves/Schmidt team. This scheme was then recommended to the owners. Jury remarks for each of the five proposals follow.

Graves/Schmidt

The jury found this design concept most appealing in the timeless quality of the site plan and its integration into the landscape. It embodies a celebration of the lifestyle that is unique to the Napa Valley. The collaboration between artist and architect is classically blended into the design–art as architecture and architecture as art.

The overall design plan resembles that of a village. Each element–the winery, sculpture garden, and residence–is articulated yet woven into a common cloth with many patterns. The winery is well conceived and functionally delineated in a way that clearly defines public and industrial functions. The plan could be phased, and the individual forms defining spaces could be incrementally realized while remaining part of the overall composition.

The procession through the various winery functions, eventually leading to the sculpture garden, is well integrated into the site.

The imagery embodied in the design and the complexity of the experience for the visitor are appropriate to the actual making of wine. If this design were to be built, the jury recommended that there be no compromise in the quality of craftsmanship and materials so as to insure the integrity of the design.

The residence, while a part of the complex, is removed and private in itself–a container for living that is set gracefully within the gardens. Both the residence and garden have a sense of history and classicism, presenting a literal but sensitive response to the requested design program.

Recognizing there is a certain "style" inherent in this proposal, the jury has looked beyond the esthetic to determine the essence of the design. The site development plan is a brilliant piece of work. It segregates public functions from private; recognizes service/vehicular functions as distinct requirements; creates opportunities for discovery, adventure, and invention; and has a poetic complexity that will age well.

In recommending this design concept to the owner, the jury congratulates the design team and commends them for their work. This design should be built as a demonstration of a commitment to excellence–in wine, in art, in architecture.

Mangurian/Turrell

The jury was impressed with the myriad of ideas presented here. The proposal demonstrates a compatible relationship of spirit between the artist and architect–they are searching for the same mysteries. It is also the most courageous and spiritual of the entries... it challenged the jury by showing what could be.

The jury felt the linearity of the plan was both an asset and a liability. It sets up a processional effect that is almost religious in nature. The incorporation of asymmetry for certain functions might add to the richness of the scheme.

The forecourt of water creates a horizontal landmark.

The winery courtyard is a theater, acting out the process of wine making. The courtyard is almost medieval in character and an illustrative approach to marketing wine. The jury questions, however, the advisability of providing storage functions between the forecourt and the courtyard, and the possibility of conflict between the transferring of stored goods in cross-circulation and the arrival of new truckloads of grapes.

The subtle relationships between the courtyards of the winery and residence, the grotto, and the light tunnels are all presented as private entities that could greatly enhance the public experience of the site. The jury salutes the team's research into the use of caves for winery operations and recommends the owner take into consideration these findings.

In travelling up the knoll, complex relationships are formed between the natural landscape and man-made structures. The jury felt that the only people who would be able to fully appreciate the mysteries of the knoll would be the owners.

The jury gives high commendation to this design solution. The team dared to break new ground with this courageous presentation: without placing art within it, the complex alone stands as an example of extraordinary art.

Batey/Mack/Saari

Simplicity is difficult to achieve. Simple forms, functionally determined and then symmetrically displayed on and about a very strong axis, are a statement that can lead to elegance. The jury felt the elegance of this concept was highly dependent upon the final resolution of details and spatial delineation.

The approach to the winery is beautiful–a landmark in itself. It has the "feel" of the Napa Valley and evokes thoughts of the causeway to Mont Saint Michel. The

winery's plan is at once grand and overpowering in scale. The rich coloration proposed for the complex is indeed a strong statement–bands of color inserted into the vineyards. The technical development of the winery appears to be well executed, but the jury felt the tension that occurs between the straight and curved walls could be lost to the public.

The jury had difficulty understanding the procession of the visitor experience although the passage from the wine-tasting room along the scissor path through the follies is a romantic and delightful experience. The tower receiving the mythical Pegasus evoked a remembrance of the traditional water towers of the Napa Valley and is a provocative form in the composition.

The tactile and sensuous contribution of the artist, combined with the extreme simplicity of the model and drawings, gives this scheme a sense of timelessness. If it were built, it would be unexpectedly fragile and robust at the same time. The team is commended for its great integrity and its ability to refrain from "show business." The jury feels that if this concept were realized, it would be one of those places you happen upon and never choose to leave.

Saitowitz/Levy/O'Brien/Zimmerman

In this design scheme the entrance to both the winery and residence is unique among the proposals. Lying at the base of the knoll, the entrance treats the knoll as an archetypical form with functions applied to and around it. The granite water feature circumventing the hill and the sculpture garden path give a sense of strong delineation of the knoll.

An important element in this design is the vertical stacking of functions over the more conventional horizontal distribution. This unique plan clearly demonstrates the team's extensive knowledge of wineries. Integration with the base of the knoll and the use of berms–both as visual extensions and devices to allow vehicle access to upper levels–illustrate a unity of building with site.

The circulation of visitors through the complex is well conceived. It is at once integrated, yet separated. The exhibition of the art of wine making flows easily to the simple amphitheater–a gracious space that uses the winery as a stage set not unlike the open theaters of Elizabethan England.

The esthetic is timeless; neither daringly new nor traditionally old. The tie between the winery and residence, while each is separate, has a commonality in approach. The residence utilizes a circular form that would normally provide awkward and unusable space. The team has skillfully developed the spaces so that the form does not become overbearing but becomes a pinnacle on the knoll.

The jury found intriguing the idea of the residence, pottery studio, and winter garden as a way to further broaden the owners' experience of the knoll's natural beauty.

It is in a gentle and subtle way that this proposal is both responsive and responsible to the design program.

Solomon/Bofill/Dillon/ Stauffacher Solomon/Carpenter

Elegantly presented, this concept is alone in both its siting of the winery and its clear delineation of uses. The plan calls for the placement of the winery away from the knoll, the use of the winery's roof as a vineyard and garden above the valley floor, the conceptual line of the red-tile channel, and the setting of the house, boldly but gracefully, at the prow of the hill.

The strength of this plan is also its Achilles's heel. The development of uses into symmetrical forms and classi-

cal relationships gives the scheme a static and inflexible feeling. However, the clear definition of visitor and worker areas within and around the winery, the material selection, the "trellis" terminations of the winery, the entry ponds and bridges, and the easy procession from the entrance to the rooftop tasting room are all concepts executed with great skill. The stroll through the vineyards along the red channel–and the use of the channel as an ordering device in the scheme– are delightful ideas. A large bench hugs the circumference of the base of the knoll providing a viewing platform of the vineyards and sculpture garden.

The presentation includes a statement that collaboration on this concept transcends standard disciplinary bounds. Architect, landscape architect, and artist combined to develop this outstanding work. The jury recognized, through this presentation, that it is possible to collaborate in such a manner that the individual disciplines become fully integrated into a cohesive and functional whole.

The jury congratulates the team for its approach in satisfying the quantitative aspects of the design program. The concept and the presentation techniques have a clarity and strength that describe a complex of excellence.

The Clos Pegase Design Competition
Design Program

General

Clos Pegase will be a special place. It will be a commercial operation of quality, yet provide the privacy and solitude desired by its owners. Although a landmark, it will be integrated with a very fragile site. It must demonstrate the very highest in architectural design excellence, yet not overpower the art and the craft of wine making. It must be practical, yet romantic. These dichotomies must be addressed in the design.

The site provides both unique opportunities and constraints. Currently divided into the north and south sector by a public road, the north sector is dominated by a heavily wooded knoll atop which is a burned-out ruin of the former house. A long lane winds up the knoll from the main road to the residential site. The lower portion of the knoll provides an opportunity for a winery and circulation areas. The wooded knoll is envisioned as the site of the sculpture garden, providing the transition between the commercial aspects of the winery and the private seclusion of the residence.

The top of the knoll is the residential site. All portions of the existing ruins will be removed, and there is an opportunity to recontour or flatten the top of the knoll to gain additional building area. The knoll may be relandscaped as necessary to integrate the three major functions: the winery, the sculpture garden, and the residence.

Because of the circulation and parking requirements of the winery complex, the owner realizes that certain vineyard portions of the northern sector will be utilized for these functions. It is of prime importance that the commercial and public endeavors of the operation have the proper functional requirements and relationships as presented in the Design Program.

The Winery

The winery is to serve as a landmark and signpost for Clos Pegase. It is to be located in a visually prominent position from Highway 29. Production will eventually be 50,000 cases of wine per year with sixty percent of the wine white and forty percent red. At full capacity, a total of approximately 800 tons of grapes will be delivered to the winery each harvest during a six-week period in September and October. Daily tonnage

received may be as much as sixty tons. Total winery capacity will be approximately 300,000 gallons made up of stainless steel tanks and barrels.

Because present percolation tests allow Clos Pegase an initial winery use permit of 23,000 cases and the ultimate aim is 50,000 cases, the winery must be built in two stages, the second stage being built within five years after the first one is operational. The design should include the 50,000 case capacity, showing the separate phases of development.

The winery will be designed to display an extensive painting collection with the exhibition spaces integrated with those production facilities that are accessible to the public. Its style is open to the designer's intentions, bearing in mind only the owner's inclination toward simple materials: wood, stone, or brick. While the overall design may be monumental, it should retain simple geometric forms; in feeling it would relate to the landscape and, of course, to the spirit of the wine tradition. The latter should be particularly pertinent to the tasting and public rooms where traditional implements of wine culture from previous centuries will be displayed. The owner has envisioned a water feature tied to the public spaces of the winery.

A comment by the owner: "Its design [the winery] could easily be in the spirit of Mario Botta's Casa Rotonda, a cylinder sliced by light in two; it could also be the extreme opposite in style, Junzo Yoshimura's simple forms based on traditional ancient Japanese lines as seen in the roof of the Ise shrine complex; or it could embody the art of Arata Isozaki, a soaring temple of wood in the Japanese Alps."

Specific design requirements are as follows:

1. Relative positions and flows between process areas are presented in Diagram I. Forklift movement must be possible between all areas of the winery including the barrel storage.

2. Grape and supply trucks will be at least tractor-trailer type with trailers up to seventy feet in length. Adequate space must be provided for straight approach and exit to crusher-stemmer and grape delivery

Table I

23,000 Case Winery Space Requirements

Area no. ref. Diag. I	Area Description	Minimum Ceiling Height (ft.)	Area Perimeter (ft.)	Area sq. ft.
1	Grape Receiving & Crushing	NA	30 x 60	1,800
2	Fermenting & Processing	18	60 x 65	3,900
3	Processing	12	20 x 24	480
4	Wood Tank Room	18	30 x 80	2,400
5	Barrel Storage	12	60 x 100	6,000
6	Bottling Room	9.5	22 x 24	528
7	Bottles & Supplies Storage	18	80 x 50	4,000
8	Cased Goods Storage	18	65 x 100	6,500
9	Laboratory	8	20 x 20	400
9A	Production Tasting Room	8	20 x 20	400
10	Shop, Maintenance & Tools	8	20 x 25	500
11	Mech. Systems Room, Hot Wtr., Elect. & Refrg.	10	20 x 25	500
12	Bathrooms, Lockers, Employee Lounge	8	Design Option	1,000
13	Tasting & Dining Area	10	Design Option	1,500
13A	Kitchen	10	Design Option	750
14	Offices (Open Space Type) & Conference Room	8	Design Option	1,500

Total Area 32,158

station. The road must have an all-weather surface. Grape unloading areas must have surface elevation higher than the crush area floor elevation. Loading docks for the storage area should be provided. Truck loading and unloading surface area must be suitable for hard tire forklift traffic. The clearance needed at the site of the trucks and alternate drive locations are shown on Diagram I. The recommended maximum grade of all roads to and from the winery is eight percent.

3. The grape receiving and crush pad (Area 1) is sized for forklift operation, pumps, grape conveyor, and a crusher-stemmer. This area may be located outside, but adjacent to the winery buildings.

4. The fermentation and pressing area (Area 2) is inside the winery building. This space will contain twenty-two 113.55 HL tanks that are ninety-inches diameter and 114-inches tall; ten 151.4 HL tanks, eighty-four-inches diameter and 167-inches tall; and five 75.7 HL tanks, sixty-seven-inches diameter and 131-inches tall.

5. The wood tank room will contain twenty-five 151.4 HL tanks, eighty-four-inches diameter and 167-inches tall; five 75.7 tanks, sixty-seven-inches diameter and 131-inches tall; and one 113.6 HL tank, ninety-inches diameter and 114-inches tall.

6. In the process area (Area 3) there will be two filters, a barrel washing station, and other process equipment like centrifuges. This area must be centrally located with access to the fermentation tank area, oak tank area, barrel storage, and bottling line. This area will have considerable forklift traffic and will also be used to store pumps and other portable process equipment.

7. The laboratory (Area 9) should be at the same elevation as the production area. Natural light in this room is desirable but not absolutely necessary. The production tasting room should be adjacent to the laboratory or above if the laboratory is on the ground floor. It should have substantial northern light.

8. The mechanical room (Area 11) houses a 100-ton refrigeration system, a five HL tank, and a hot water boiler, either oil or gas fired.

9. Insulation requirement for all buildings is R = 20

minimum for walls and R = 30 minimum for roofs.

10. The tasting room (Area 13) and bathroom (Area 8) may be on the second floor level. Separate bathrooms for the general public and staff personnel are required with lockers provided in the staff facilities. All bathrooms must meet the handicapped requirements of the local Building Code.

11. As much as possible, free-spanned space should be designed for all production areas. This is especially important in the wood tank room and the warehouse, bottle storage (Area 7), and cased goods storage (Area 8). There should be no columns in the bottling room (Area 6) and process room (Area 3).

12. The warehouse space (Area 8) must be air-conditioned and run off the 100-ton refrigeration system. It must be able to be closed off from the rest of the production areas. The same is true of the wood tank room (Area 4). This room and the barrel storage area require a thirty to fifty percent humidity air space.

13. Economically unfeasible for modern wineries, gravity flow is not required or encouraged; however, linear flow from grape to bottle may be a design consideration.

14. Since the winery will conduct tours during working hours, the design concept should include tour paths and viewing areas that will not disturb any of the production operations. Areas to be toured are 1, 2, 3, 4, 5, and 6 shown in Diagram I.

15. The kitchen in Area 13A will be used for special functions only.

16. Area requirements for the Phase I case winery and the ultimate 50,000 case winery are included in the Table I and Table II following.

17. The most economical way to store barrels is to nest them. They should be nested four rows high, approximately nine to ten feet, with a ceiling height of approximately two feet above the highest barrel. Please note that in all wine storage areas, tank, barrel, or bottle, the ratio of free-air volume to container volume must be kept to a minimum.

Table II

50,000 Case Winery Space Requirements

Area no. ref. Diag. I	Area Description	Minimum Ceiling Height (ft.)	Area Perimeter (ft.)	Area sq. ft.
1	Grape Receiving & Crushing	NA	30 x 60	1,800
2	Fermenting & Processing	18	60 x 135	8,100
3	Processing	12	20 x 24	480
4	Wood Tank Room	18	60 x 80	4,800
5	Barrel Storage	12	60 x 167	10,000
6	Bottling Room	9.5	22 x 24	528
7	Bottles & Supplies Storage	18	80 x 100	8,000
8	Cased Goods Storage	18	100 x 135	13,500
9	Laboratory	8	20 x 20	400
9A	Production Tasting Room	8	20 x 20	400
10	Shop, Maintenance & Tools	8	20 x 25	500
11	Mech. Systems Room, Hot Wtr., Elect. & Refrg.	10	20 x 25	500
12	Bathrooms, Lockers, Employee Lounge	8	Design Option	1,000
13	Tasting & Dining Area	10	Design Option	1,500
13A	Kitchen	10	Design Option	750
14	Offices (Open Space Type) & Conference Room	8	Design Option	1,500

Total Area 53,758

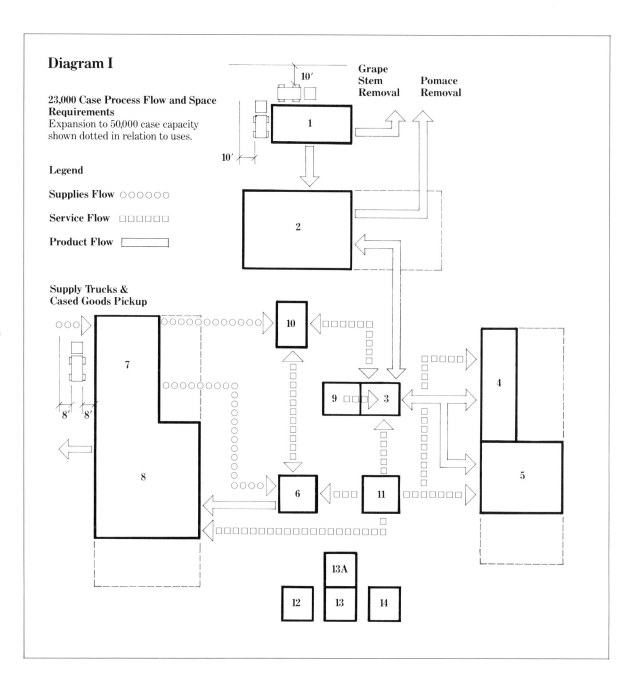

Diagram I

23,000 Case Process Flow and Space Requirements
Expansion to 50,000 case capacity shown dotted in relation to uses.

Legend

Supplies Flow ○○○○○○

Service Flow ☐☐☐☐☐☐

Product Flow ▭

Grape Stem Removal

Pomace Removal

Supply Trucks & Cased Goods Pickup

The Sculpture Garden

The sculpture garden is intended to become a landscaped park open to the public. It is to contain, within its topographical limitations, a water element, lawns, flower beds, and a walking path that meanders through its ever-growing contemporary sculpture collection. If feasible, it could contain a small open-air theater for informal musical and theatrical performances.

The sculpture collection will be avant-garde and eclectic, concentrating on recent works, primarily American. It will initially be endowed with a small nucleus of key works including, among others, works by Arp, Cesar's giant bronze thumb, and two black signals by Takis standing fifteen to twenty feet high. The collection will grow constantly by new acquisitions, some of which will consist of site-specific commissions.

The garden is clearly the least defined facility in the Design Program. This is intentional. The spirit, ceremony, procession, and character of the garden are seen as the "glue" that cements the commercial operation to the residence and marries the entire complex to the site. It should have security provisions, flexible settings for art, and a unique experience of art in nature.

While not a specific requirement, the garden should include sites and locations for ten major "focal" pieces or events, plus have the ability to accept innumerable minor pieces throughout. The sites should be varied, presenting locations against the sky, in and around water, in glades—all providing a continuous sequence of experiences.

The owner expects major relandscaping of the knoll to occur, and is prepared for major tree removal if called for in the design. Water is available for ponds or water features from a private reservoir in the south parcel.

The Residence

The owners are a mature, cosmopolitan couple with two teenage children. They have enjoyed a culturally rich life, living for extended periods of time both in Tokyo and Paris. They envision their new residence to have the image of a classical villa that blends the best of both the East and the West into the unique environment of the Napa Valley.

The residence should be set in a series of gardens, of which the largest is the surrounding vineyards. Procession, anticipation, and surprise form the sequence approaching the house from the entry gates. Orchards, colonnades, ponds, pavilions, and courts can be utilized in the site planning. Major rooms opening onto special gardens (flower, vegetable, lawn) are desirable.

While we previously stated in the submission package that the residence's main theme should be its rustic aspect, the word "rustic" may have been incorrectly interpreted. While the owners are open to most styles that fit within their constraints, they envision large ceramic squares in the living room and dining room, with wood and other natural material predominating throughout.

While allowing utmost space for paintings, the interior should be built around an atrium, have a covered winter garden, one large living room, a study, four bedrooms, a pottery workshop, and a Japanese bath overlooking its own enclosed garden. Ceiling heights in the living room should be at least fifteen feet and ten feet in the rest of the house. Some of the bedrooms may be on a second floor.

The main window of every room should face as near to south as possible to have the full benefits of the sun. Calistoga summers are hotter than the rest of Napa, and the winters colder. While air-conditioning will be required, it will be used sparingly as the owners do not favor it. The house must have the maximum insulation from the sun in summer while obtaining maximum exposure to it in winter.

The owners have fond remembrances of their home overlooking Paris, built by Napoleon for one of his marshals. The owners also admire the Japanese architectural concept in which there is a sense of simplicity and a desire to achieve a fusion with nature, yielding what can be described as a house composed of three parts: exterior, intermediate, and interior. The exterior is symbolized by the garden, and the interior by the main living areas. The intermediate area is an important buffer between these two and helps to draw nature into the house while still providing protection. While this architecture was born out of the need to draw in the breeze during Japan's predominantly hot and humid summers and rainy spring and fall seasons, the three parts could be adapted to a home where humidity is not a problem by yielding open, airy vistas, walls and corners where two glass panels meet without the obstruction of a corner post, and verandas and atriums that bring the garden into the house.

The owners presently reside in a contemporary house in San Francisco designed by Joseph Esherick as well as one built before Versailles in Paris and are comfortable in both. While disliking the coldness which comes from too much metal and glass, they have an open mind regarding the style of their future residence in the Napa Valley.

Addendum

The following items are clarifications to the Design Program dated 7/9/84 and the Regulations dated 5/1/84, resulting from the Precompetition Meeting held 9 July 1984. They are hereby incorporated as part of the Design Program and the Regulations.

1. Modifications and Additions to the Design Program

1.1 Parking: for the purposes of the competition, the requirement is fifteen public spaces and ten staff spaces, associated jointly with the winery and sculpture garden.

1.2 Waste Water Treatment Ponds: two ponds of equal size, each having a potential depth of ten feet including two-feet freeboard, each with a land area of approximately one-half acre, approximately square or circular in shape. One pond will be required for each phase of development (23,000 cases and 50,000 cases). Ponds are to be located on the north parcel and treated water can be used for irrigation on the knoll.

1.3 The existing water cistern shall be retained at the top of the knoll but may be moved to another location at the top of the knoll to allow for more freedom in the layout of the residence.

1.4 Page 9 of 11, fifth paragraph, delete "reservoir in the south parcel" and replace with "well at the base of the knoll."

1.5 Page 10 of 11, fifth paragraph, delete the sentence "The main window of every room should face as near to south as possible to take the full benefits of the sun." To the fifth paragraph, add a final sentence: "The owners prefer a southern exposure and view where practicable.

The Finalists

Team Members
Andrew Batey
Mark Mack
Peter Saari
Frank Frost
Wendy Tsuji
Hassan Afrookhteh
Klaus Kiesler
Reza Hadaegh
Alex Usvitsky
Maya Lin
William Rose
David Hall
Ann Kirschner

The house, the sculpture garden, and the winery are an integrated piece: together they transform the site into something greater.

The winery is a straightforward, practical, and economical solution to making wine, at the same time recognizing the need for a romantic atmosphere. This is achieved in scale, material, and dramatic sequence.

The sculpture garden uses the knoll as its generator and can be as gentle an experience as a walk along a path, or as exciting as probing a misty grotto. The entire knoll becomes the signpost for Clos Pegase. The house is simple in form and plan, organized around a valley life of informal enjoyment of nature, work, and pleasant social intercourse.

The public sequence is as follows: car entry at south end of property–drive along concourse elevated between ponds–then left alongside ramp building to the park area–walk up ramp to roof of building–cross over internal winery road via bridge into tasting room–on through center of cylinder to beginning of sculpture garden walk–switchback from folly to folly to destination.

The private sequence is from house through courtyard and to pool–down into secret stairway through the penultimate folly into the sculpture garden or down to the pottery studio and along a path again into the garden.

The work-a-day sequence is entry at the second gatehouse between winery buildings, check-in and/or weigh-in at gatehouse, then on road between buildings.

The buildings are constructed of substantial, energy-saving materials–thick walls of block rendered or exposed of simple proportions–easy to construct and configured to take advantage of the climate. The winery is built into the hill to conserve heat gain on the long wall–and roofed with three inches of water to insulate and decorate.

The winery buildings are climbed over or pierced. Parking during the first phase occurs behind the ramps–and upon completion of the extremities of the front (dry) building. The rotunda is a dramatic enclosure which serves as an amphitheater housing temporary valley events. It is entered from above via the ramps. The cross-over allows viewing exterior winery functions from above and entry into the public tasting area.

The "dry" building is cased goods and bottle storage only–with mechanical systems centered and accessible to the other buildings via ducts under the bridge. The "wet" building contains barrel and tank storage–bottling, processing, lab, etc. The base of the cylinder is semiopen, housing the variety of winery tasks, the second floor houses all official endeavors, and the top, the public and ceremonial. All levels are accessible by elevator, dumbwaiter, and stairways. The walls of the cylinder–the solid of the rotunda–void will be lined with art on the second and third levels–the gentle curvature uninterrupted for this purpose.

One may continue onward through the heart of the cylinder onto the hill and beyond back and forth through the sculpture garden. Each extremity is a sculpture site. The first is a deep cave oozing cool waters from the stream above; the second a neo-classical grotto of enormous stone; the next a minimalist maze; the fourth a wine-tasting folly; the fifth a semicircular backdrop for a dramatic large sculpture. At this stage the garden is a specific path but a loose one, and allowance has been made for more paths and meanders so that this is a blueprint for a more elaborate garden–when pieces are added, new areas and frames can be inserted.

The house is organized around a large view embracing the courtyard. It is entered from a lower level by car through the garage, or by a massive staircase across from guest parking. The stairs land at a gallery entry–the focal point for the collections wrapping around the house on its southern exposure. All rooms are configured around the gallery and buffered from one another by thick walls. One roof is accessible for more spectacular views and sun protection below the exuberant trellis.

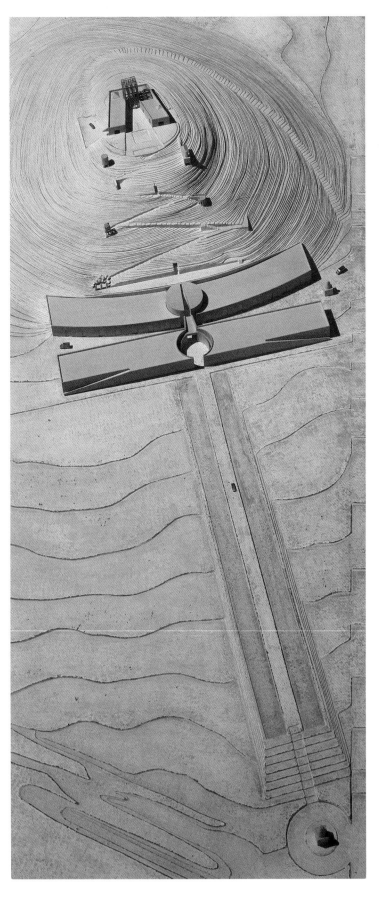

Model, 1984
plaster, cork, and wood
10 x 27 x 60″ (25.4 x 68.6 x 152.4)

Sketch, 1984, ink and watercolor on linen mounted on masonite, 30 x 40″ (76.2 x 101.6)

Elevation, 1984
ink and watercolor on linen mounted on masonite
30 x 40″ (76.2 x 101.6)

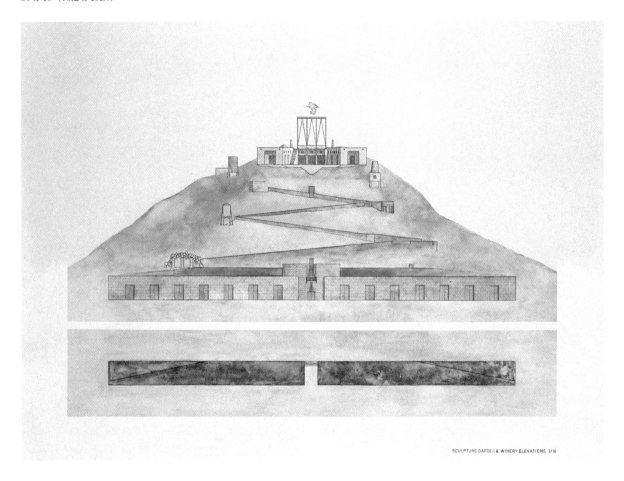

SCULPTURE GARDEN & WINERY ELEVATIONS 1/16

36

Peter Saari
Frontal View: Surface Study
plaster and gesso on masonite
12 x 108″ (30.5 x 274.3)

Plan of Winery and Sculpture Garden, 1984
ink and watercolor on linen mounted on masonite
30 x 40″ (76.2 x 101.6)

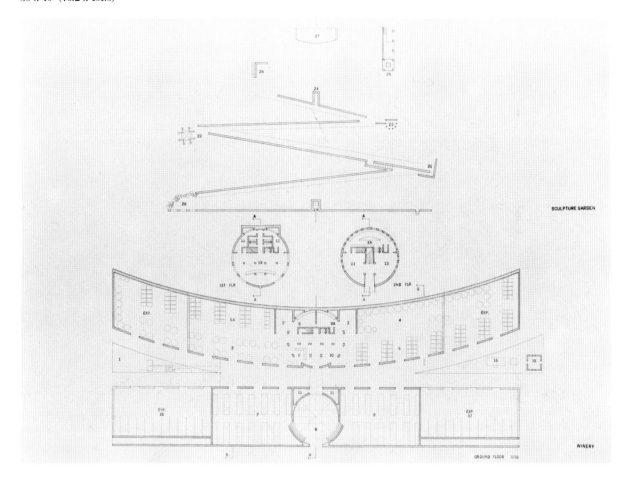

HOUSE ELEVATIONS 1/8

House Elevations, 1984
ink on linen mounted on masonite
30 x 40″ (76.2 x 101.6)

This super-scaled object crowns the hill with appropriate scale to the entire complex–a landing pad awaiting the visit of Pegasus.

The house is a modest, low-slung structure–simple in geometry and character but sturdy–built of block with deep cuts for openings. The kind of form which invites aging–vines crawling upon its surface, emphasizing light and shadow–the play of time. It doesn't compete with the landscape, nor does it signal a "style" or period. Timeless and solid.

The construction of the winery is state-of-the-art economic building technique: tilt-up construction slab walls with plaster cladding on the "dry" building and stone on the "wet." Spans are maximized and simplified by prefab trusses with built-up roofs. The "dry" is decked over with a polymer system and the "wet" likewise, and then flooded with three inches of water for increased insulation and a cool pleasant vista from the house above.

The three different entrances are clearly defined and constitute a hierarchy in sequence. First the public at the southern extremity with its gatehouse and powerful axial view across the vineyard to the center of the winery and sculpture garden–all seen at a glance from the road. Next the working entry with its gatehouse and a peek into the no-nonsense slit between the winery buildings–and finally the understated private entrance to the house and the secrets further up the hill.

The artist-architect collaboration was thought of in terms of the building form and building fabric–the facade shape as Pegasus wings–and its material as slowly, gracefully aging plaster– a majestic artwork recalling ancient structures. The artist has determined the quality and nature of the facade material as well as individual pieces within the sculpture garden. The facade manifestation is a representation of the artist's notion of layering and aging, and coloration.

Andrew Batey

Mark Mack

Andrew Batey was born in Merced, California, in 1944. He was educated at Occidental College, Los Angeles (B.A., 1966); the University of Oxford, England, where he received his diploma in the history of art (1968); and at the University of Cambridge, England (M. Arch., 1971). He worked with Norman Foster in London from 1971 to 1972 and with Andreas Casillas and Luis Barragan in Mexico City during 1973 to 1976. In 1978, he established the firm of Batey & Mack in San Francisco with Mark Mack. Well known for residential work, the firm's projects include the Holt residence, Corpus Christi, Texas (1982), the Hildebrandt residence, Oakville, California (1983), and the Rodino residence, Calistoga, California (1984). Batey & Mack was recently commissioned to design the interiors and furniture for the J. Paul Getty Museum's Center for the History of Art, Santa Monica, California.

The work of Batey & Mack has been featured in various exhibitions including the Venice Biennale, 1980; *California Counterpoint: Architecture 1982*, organized by the Institute for Architecture and Urban Studies, New York, and the San Francisco Art Institute (travelled, catalog published); and *Follies*, 1983, held at Leo Castelli Gallery, New York (travelled, catalog published).

Batey has been a visiting lecturer at the University of California (Berkeley and Los Angeles); Southern California Institute of Architecture, Santa Monica; Princeton University, New Jersey; and the University of Pennsylvania, Philadelphia. He is a founder and editor of *Archetype*, a West Coast journal of architecture and other arts.

He currently resides in Yountville, California.

Mark Mack was born in Judenberg, Austria, in 1949. He attended the Hoherer Techniche Leranstalt für Hochbau in Graz, Austria, from 1963 to 1968 and entered the master class of Professor Dr. Roland Rainer at the Akademie der bildenden Kunste in Vienna in 1969. During the period before graduation in 1973, he worked for Steiger & Partners, Zurich, and Atelier Hans Hollein, Vienna. After coming to the United States in 1973, he worked for Hausrucker Inc., New York, on the Rooftop Oasis project, a study funded by the National Endowment for the Arts on the suitability of New York City rooftops for habitation, leisure, and cultural activities. From 1975 to 1976 Mack worked for Emilio Ambasz, New York, on projects including a proposal to transform a Grand Rapids, Michigan, post office into a cultural center which won a *Progressive Architecture* award in 1976, and the 1976 Venice Biennale. After moving to the Bay Area in 1976, Mack worked as a freelance architect and renderer and established Western Addition, a nonprofit organization committed to innovative ideas in architecture which sponsored lectures by local and internationally recognized architects. In 1978, he joined Andrew Batey to found Batey & Mack, and in 1979 they began publishing *Archetype* where he remains an editor. Since 1981, Mack has been a visiting lecturer at the University of California, Berkeley. He has lectured widely throughout the United States and Canada.

He currently resides in San Francisco.

Selected Bibliography for Batey & Mack
Archer, B.J. *Follies: Architecture for the Late-Twentieth-Century Landscape.* New York: Rizzoli, 1983.
California Counterpoint: Architecture 1982. New York: Institute for Architecture and Urban Studies and Rizzoli, 1982.
Gandee, C.K. "Villa on the Bay, Corpus Christi, Texas." *Architectural Record* 172 (Mid-April 1984): 96-103.
"Knipschild Residence [Napa Valley, California]." *Progressive Architecture* 65 (January 1984): 110-111.
"Primitive Modernism." *Studio International* 195 (June 1982): 39-43.

Peter Saari was born in New York in 1951. He studied at the School of Visual Arts, New York, and the Tyler School of Art in Rome. He received his B.F.A. from C.W. Post College, Long Island University, in 1974 and his M.F.A. from Yale University, New Haven, Connecticut, in 1976. Saari creates the "aged" effect of classical Mediterranean frescoes in his imitative surfaces made entirely of acrylic and plaster on shaped canvas. His first one-person show was held at Lamagna Gallery, New York, in 1974. Subsequent solo exhibitions include O.K. Harris Works of Art, New York, in 1977, 1978, 1980, 1981, and 1985. His work was included in *Directions*, 1979, organized by the Hirshhorn Museum and Sculpture Garden, Smithsonian Institution, Washington, D.C. (catalog published), and *Contemporary Trompe L'Oeil Painting and Sculpture*, 1983, Boise Gallery of Art, Idaho (travelled, catalog published). Among his commissions is a ceiling mural for the Crown Building, New York.

He currently resides in Short Hills, New Jersey.

Selected Bibliography
Batey, Andrew. "Peter Saari." *Archetype* 1 (Spring 1979): 33-34.
Becker, Robert. "My Life in Ruins." *Interview* (August 1981): 40-41.
Blau, Douglas. "Reviews." *Artforum* 18 (Summer 1980): 86-87.
Clark, John R. "The Reality of Illusion." *Arts Magazine* 55 (February 1981): 158.
Donnell-Kotrozo, Carol. "Material Illusion: On the Issue of Ersatz Objects." *Arts Magazine* 58 (1984): 88-94.

Peter Saari

Mangurian/Turrell

Team Members
Robert Mangurian
James Turrell
Design Team
Ajax
Jean Bellman
Tom Buresh
Danelle Guthrie
Mitchell Lawrence
Susan Nardulli
Dan Rhodes
Natalie Richards
Ken Saylor
Molly Schneider
Katie Spitz
Consultants
Landscape Architecture
Pamela Burton
Mechanical Engineering
Jerry Sullivan
Structural Engineering
Eugene Birnbaum

**Mangurian/Turrell
Competition Statement**

This competition statement was submitted in the form of
a conversation between the artist and architect. The following
are excerpts from that exchange.

Artist: …Basically I think that our work together has dealt
with both working inside and outside, and with inside allowing
outside in, and with enclosures that are also completely open
to the outside and basically in the outside. In this tunnel area,
what we're doing is having a tunnel that faces due east and due
west with a slight upward grade so that it catches the sun just
after it's risen and just before it sets on one day of the year, the
day of the equinox. The light then comes through the tunnel
twice a year and twice a day on that equinox day, once in the
morning and once in the evening, so four times a year this is
marked, and the sun enters the tunnel, say on the equinox
morning, and the light is reflected underneath the house up
onto the floor, and there's actually a hydrogen-alpha filter so that
you can see the surface of the sun and flares, and this is right
into the surface of the floor. This image comes in and stays there
for several minutes and then it disappears. Then in the evening
of the same day, just as the sun is setting, it does the same thing
again. This is one of the markings of time. At the same time it's
a very interesting marking. It's not at the extremes, that is, the
summer solstice or winter solstice, but is a little more of an
intellectual exact middle. I think the equinox is a very interesting day because it's the day when day equals night.…

This vaulted tunnel or corridor that goes from the outside of
this portion into the courtyard is barrel-vaulted and in fact has
a slot at the top.… As the sun rises from the east, we're looking
north, so it would be from the right that, as it gets toward its
zenith, there is a moment when hard light from the sun is
allowed to come through the slot all the way to the floor. What
happens is that the first moment the light enters the space it is
a very tiny sliver, a line of the floor to wall join, and that's the
first time that light is allowed to enter.… Then it goes toward
solar noon, and this sliver of light begins to move in the opposite
direction from left to right across the floor. As it moves toward
the center of the floor, it increases in width until, at solar noon,

Model, 1984
plaster and pigment on plywood
12 x 60 x 60″ (30.5 x 152.4 x 152.4)

it is at the center, and the line on the floor is at its widest and the same width as the slot above. Then this line continues to wipe to the right as the sun goes toward the west until it decreases in size as it goes toward the wall, until it becomes this tiny sliver against the right wall, or east wall. And then disappears.

Architect: Magically.

Artist: Of course. That's how this space works, and it's another marking of time, more temporal a marking of daily time as opposed to this yearly time that's being marked up in the tunnel, where the image of the sun is coming into the house twice a year on two days of the year.

Architect: And then probably we might just jump up to the house and say that the two arcades on the east and west side of the house facing the courtyard have the same phenomena occurring.

Artist: In the house, at the southern end of the court, is where the image of the sun appears, and it's appearing at the equinox so it's having this yearly marking on each side of the court in a barrel-vaulted archway, and in that area it's doing this marking of time during the day with the same wiping of the line. Then at the top is this one spot that's actually essentially telling time on the north side of the court throughout the day.

Architect: Sort of a pinhole thing....

Artist: And then in the bedroom, we're working with the lunar cycles or the moon cycles. There is one space that completely does the sun throughout the day and throughout the year, and there's another that's marking the monthly cycles of the moon. That's in the bedroom and is out of the way from this area that works with the reflecting pool that we're making....

Architect: The stairs surrounding the courtyard, the large steps, and the loading dock, are all a red color, a red iron oxide you find in the soil in the area. And the columns and walls and underside of the overhanging roof are yellow ochre, also an earth pigment. Both colors enhance the blueness of the sky.

Artist: Yes, the one thing that this courtyard is doing is that as you're in it, the careful knife edge of the courtyard that allows you to see no thickness tends to bring this space of the sky down to the limits of the space of the courtyard that you are in, and then the tone of this slight ochre white or off-white tends to increase the intensity of the blueness, as it complements the color of the blue sky. Then at night, or actually at twilight or dawn, this is intensified by the lighting of the underside of this partial roof. It actually does change the color of the sky. The manner in which this works is that we tend to read surfaces by what their colors are, and not the manner in which they're lighted, so if you see a whiter surface, and it's lighted with tungsten light, or it's lighted with quartz halogen or fluorescent white light, we tend to see that surface still as white, even though in fact it is colored differently by each of these different lights on it, so we tend to read the surface more than we read the light coming off of it. By doing this, something does have to change, and what changes is the color of the sky, so that actually the light in this space will literally change the color of the sky.

Architect: It will actually enhance the sunsets.

Artist: And this really happens as it gets away from noon, more toward dawn, or more toward sunset. Now, at night, the light on the interior when seen from above has a certain color tone. Because of this the knife edge seems to be like a pool of light, almost like seeing light in a swimming pool, but when you're down inside it, the light that's in the interior space literally alters what you can see in the sky in the same way that when you light an area of the city sky at night, you take away the vision of stars. This lighting of the interior of the courtyard makes an extreme black, so that you really see few stars. Now you will see a few more than you will see in the top courtyard because the top courtyard will have the most intense quality, the most intense black of any of the spaces, so that as you go up, the light in the pools is gentle and then it increases in intensity in its ability to hold the volume as you go from the bottom up to the top, and that's how the spaces are structured in the lighting....

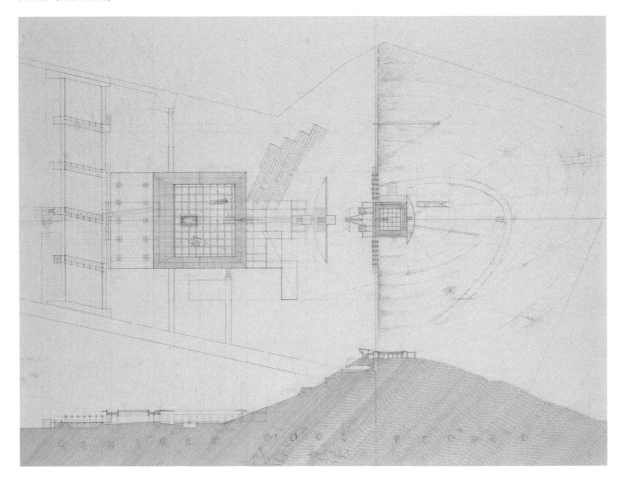

In the sky wall room, as you enter it, you see only sky because
it's above the horizon and it's this very flat surface with a pyra-
mid of steps right below it that don't go up to the top of it.
They're one step below, as in the sky space courtyard that was
just exited. The paratron of light that is in there will actually
change and work the color in the sky so that it picks up these
often opaque hues that come in and close off the space. The
space is in fact entirely open but it does make enclosure, and
this enclosure changes by the quality of the light. It's much like

light that is regulated for visual penetration on stage. You can see the things on the stage, but you can't after you see the audience. Or when you're at a lectern, the same thing, just a very small amount of light near you controls the penetration of your vision, so that in fact you literally make enclosure without having form enclose you. So on this one it does much the same except it's doing it on a surface that is vertical as opposed to the horizontal surface above you as in the sky space of the courtyard....

Architect: It amuses while using the knife edge.

Artist: Yes, the wall is slightly curved and the knife edge is worked so that you really can't see it until you're up on the stairs. Maybe it's a little bit before that.

Architect: The large arch also emanates from the radius, emanates from the sun on the spot.

Artist: Oh, that spot is the one to which the knife edge wall is directed. Oh, that's wonderful.

Architect: It looks basically northeast which is quite a big orientation. When you start walking up the stairs you begin to see the hills around, and those are lit, especially all during the day.

Artist: As you step up these steps then, the scene below rises in the opening. This becomes a special entrance. Actually you can step through the opening. It is in fact a stair, and then there are stairs that run through like a stile, come slightly down the other side of it, and take you down the hill but at the level of the top of the brush, not down in it, but you're walking on the top of the chaparral layer. Down into this area, you connect to the arc that goes from northeast back to due west that is the level of the equinox tunnel.

Architect: That little walkway that is on the contour line itself, connecting from the bottom of the stair to the tunnel, actually comes along halfway, and shifts about four feet, so that you can call it the Devil's Walk. If you continue walking you'd just fall off into the hill, but if you stop and make that four-foot adjustment then you can continue walking on the path. That's quite nice, and it's one of the seven mysteries. That side of the hill marked by the equinox tunnel is pretty much cleaned up and thinned out somewhat. It has the same dense vegetation as it has now and within it are these seven spots or seven mysteries, which will remain a mystery. Another one of the quite nice things is the large Indian mounds that go as bumps in the earth over the road.

Artist: Just like a large snake. That's going to be very nice.

Architect: It then wanders down basically ending up at the northwest corner where that open triangle of land is. Hopefully these mysteries would just emerge in a sense in the forest on that north side of the hill, as you wandered around there. And those are quite private experiences, I think.

I was thinking this morning that there's a counterpart to those experiences which are the seven mysteries, which would be the seven, let's say, installations on the south side of the hill by a series of artists....

One of the other features of the house is the bedroom located on that northwest part of that arced building that's connected to the courtyard. In that bedroom, sitting on your bed which is again two feet down from the courtyard level, you would look out and on that access would be the pool. It thins out to this narrow pool which overhangs the hill.

Artist: And we're doing it that way so that it also reflects the complete horizon.

Architect: So that has no edge to it, it's just a pool.

Artist: The water rolls right over the edge so that its miniscus reflects the horizon.

Architect: Also you look out from that room and basically have a spectacular view of all the mountains on the east side, which are all lit from south and west light. Especially Mount St. Helena.

Now from that bedroom, or little anteroom entering the bedroom, there's a stair that goes down into the ground.

Artist: The space is essentially like a sky space that works light from above except the edges are worked the same way completely through water. As you look up through it, you cannot see the edges of the pool–you can only see sky from anywhere you stand in the room below. But you are seeing it through this thickness of water which is about two–three feet thick.

Architect: Also that water can be lit, can't it? So that when you're looking out there you really can coordinate that water with the music playing in the room. That tunnel connecting the anteroom and the bedroom to the underground room below the pool probably is a sauna or some kind of exercise room....

Artist: The floors are going to be snowflake obsidian which, when laid out in the large patterns and polished, is this very black stone that has these little white spots in it. In fact, sometimes the snowflake obsidian really has this quality of being just like a star pattern. So it's a beautiful, extremely hard surface that would be polished. And yet it has this star quality in the bottom of it....

Architect: Yes, that actually is quite nice. Another space in the house is the prow which has the stair cutting through it going down into the bunker. The prow you can walk out on. It's really a view of everything.

Artist: That's great there.

Architect: Almost like the helm of a ship. To the west of the courtyard is one of the arcaded spaces that looks out over that cablelike gridwork which has the wisteria on it....

Well, if we do this project I'll be finding someone else to work with, there's clearly no more ideas.

Artist: We've used up all the ideas either of us will ever have....

Robert Mangurian was born in Baltimore in 1941. He was educated at Stanford University, California (1959-61), and the University of California, Berkeley (B. Arch., 1967). In 1969, he established S T U D I O- W O R K S, Venice, California, and New York, with Craig Hodgetts where he is now the principal architect. Recognized for innovative design combining classical forms with contemporary technology, S T U D I O- W O R K S's major projects include the Southside Settlement House, Columbus, Ohio (1977), which won a *Progressive Architecture* award (1981); the Market Street Gallery and residence, Venice, California (1977); and the Venice Interarts Center, California (1980), an ongoing project in which turn-of-the-century buildings, formerly the Venice City Hall and jail, will be converted into a center for the arts.

From 1969 to 1976, Mangurian taught at the School of Architecture and Urban Studies, the City College of the City University of New York, and then left to spend a year as a Fellow at the American Academy in Rome. He was a lecturer at the School of Architecture and Urban Planning at the University of California, Los Angeles, from 1975 to 1983 and is presently teaching at the Southern California Institute of Architecture, Santa Monica. Mangurian's work has been featured in exhibitions including *Excavation: South Side: Columbus*, 1980, P.S.1, New York; *California Counterpoint: Architecture 1982*, organized by the Institute for Architecture and Urban Studies, New York, and the San Francisco Art Institute (travelled, catalog published); and *12 Fragments of Architecture*, 1982, at Princeton University School of Architecture, New Jersey. His furniture has been shown in exhibitions including *Furniture by Architects: Contemporary Chairs, Tables, and Lamps*, 1982, organized by the Hayden Gallery, Massachusetts Institute of Technology, Cambridge (catalog published), and the 1983 Memphis Collection, Milan.

He currently resides in Venice, California.

Robert Mangurian

Selected Bibliography
Boissiere, C. "California: Craig Hodgetts/Robert Mangurian." *Domus* 604 (March 1980): 18-19.
California Counterpoint: Architecture 1982. New York: Institute for Architecture and Urban Studies and Rizzoli, 1982.
"Southside Settlement, A Community Facility in Columbus, Ohio." *Progressive Architecture* 52 (January 1976): 62-63.
"Venice Interarts Center, Venice, California." *Progressive Architecture* 64 (January 1983): 90-91.

James Turrell was born in Los Angeles in 1943. He was educated at Pomona College, Claremont, California (B.A. Psychology, 1965); the University of California, Irvine (1965-66) where he pursued graduate studies in art; and the Claremont Graduate School, California (M.A. Art, 1973). Following Turrell's first one-person exhibition at the Pasadena Art Museum (now the Norton Simon Museum), California, in 1967, he has had numerous solo exhibitions at institutions including the Stedelijk Museum, Amsterdam, 1976 (catalog published); Whitney Museum of American Art, New York, 1980 (catalog published); Portland Center for the Visual Arts, Oregon, 1981; the Israel Museum, Jerusalem, 1983 (catalog published); and the Musèe d'Art Moderne de la Ville de Paris, 1984 (catalog published). His awards include two National Endowment for the Arts grants (1968, 1975); a Guggenheim Fellowship (1974); and a MacArthur Foundation Fellowship (1984). Turrell's major works include a commissioned installation at the Villa Panza in Varese, Italy, for Guiseppe Panza de Biumo (1974), and the Roden Crater Project, forty-five miles northeast of Flagstaff, Arizona, where Turrell is shaping an extinct volcanic cinder cone into a natural observatory. The Museum of Contemporary Art in Los Angeles is organizing an exhibition of Turrell's work scheduled to open in November 1985.

He currently resides in Flagstaff, Arizona.

James Turrell

53

Selected Bibliography
Adcock, Craig. "Anticipating 19,084: James Turrell's Roden Crater Project." *Arts Magazine* 58 (May 1984): 76-85.
Coplans, John. "James Turrell: Projected Light Images." *Artforum* VI (October 1967): 48-49.
Gandel, Milton, "If One Hasn't Visited Count Panza's Villa, One Doesn't Really Know What Collecting Is All About." *Art News* 78 (December 1979): 44-49.
Larson, Kay. "Dividing the Light from the Darkness." *Artforum* 19 (January 1981): 30-33.
Russell, John. "James Turrell: Light and Space." *New York Times*, 31 October 1980: C22.

Team Members
Stanley Saitowitz
Toby Levy
Pat O'Brien
Elyn Zimmerman
Design Assistants
Daniel A. Luis
John Bass
Patrick Winters
Yung Ho Chang
Model Maker
Frank Wang
Model Assistants
Eric John
Miwon Kwon
Erin O'Reilly
Geoff Holton
Randy Tuell
Ross Levy
Christophe Particolar

Introduction

The hill and the buildings are reciprocal; the shape of the hill and its position to the land have determined the structures of the Clos Pegase winery, house, and sculpture garden. These structures now inform our experience of the land.

The skirt of trees which lines the base of the hill is completed on the south by the winery building. This acts as a plinth to the hill, transforming it into the building.

The top of the plinth is marked out by a row of sycamore trees. These line the sculpture walk, circling the hill at this level.

A triangular sector of the hill is cleared on the south face. This clearing connects the house and the winery, and unites the elements of art, architecture, and landscape. Columns of poplar trees form an edge to the natural growth and are pierced by the water elements which circle the hill. The house is at the crest of the hill. Its flying roof heralds Pegasus.

It is the integration of the winery, residence, and sculpture garden with its setting that will give Clos Pegase its presence in the Napa Valley landscape.

The Winery

The winery is at the base of the hill. Its building describes the wine-making process both as a factory addressing wine production and in synopsis it informs its visitor.

The building splits in the center with a series of terraces allowing the knoll to cascade to the vineyard and mark the public entry to the winery. The entry to the winery is the entry to the hill. It is a dark space recalling wine caves and cellars that leads the visitor to the tour bridge. The bridge at the first mezzanine in the wood tank room enables synoptic viewing of the fermentation tanks and barrel storage. From the bridge the tour continues via courts and terraces up the hill to the wine-tasting and dining room. The terrace at the upper level reaches back into the hill forming the amphitheater.

From the vineyard it sits in, the wine is crushed and stored in a berm of earth. It is bottled and distributed above, and tasted on the roof.

The core of services stacks densely as mezzanines at the center of the building. This fixed center allows expansion of the winery on both sides in phase two.

The thirty-foot grid organizes and reveals the wine-making process. The grid is as simple as the process it serves. From the outset, where the grapes enter in the crushing area, the grid is visible. It shelters the fermentation tanks and becomes the framework for the precast walls of the wood tank and barrel storage area. Suspended lightweight catwalks provide servicing at the mezzanine level above. The second level houses the bottling and cased goods storage and their support facilities. An additional 7,000 square feet of storage will be provided elsewhere.

As the winery rises it reduces in mass, matching the tapering of the knoll. The uppermost level of offices and wine tasting emerges into the light using its grid to capture outdoor space.

The Residence
The house crowns the hill. Its form, a circle with a triangular court cut out, reiterates the forms of the knoll with its triangular clearing. Sitting on a square base, the remaining areas form seasonal terraces and contain a site-specific water sculpture and pool.

The house is a gallery. The services are combined into cores which act as spatial dividers creating opportunities for display. The implied corridors along the court are galleries. The double volume living room is a gracious setting for large works, set against glimpses of the forest.

The thick circular wall at the rear is slit to provide ambiant light into the interior spaces. The upper level of the wall is further eroded to create exterior spaces. The Japanese bath opens

Model, 1984
walnut, basswood, sponge, paint, and foam
8½ x 27 x 60″ (21.6 x 68.6 x 152.4)

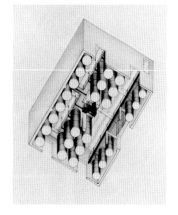
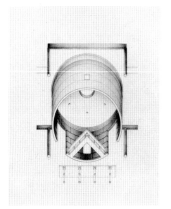

*Axonometric Drawings of Wood Tank and
Tasting Room*, 1984
ink and airbrush on vellum
30 x 40″ (76.2 x 101.6)

58

Elevation, 1984
ink and airbrush on vellum
30 x 40″ (76.2 x 101.6)

60

Elyn Zimmerman
Model Section of Water Feature, 1984
granite
5³⁄₈ x 6 x 9³⁄₄″ (14.3 x 15.2 x 24.8)

to the forest and is perched in the trees with its private deck. The courtyard elevation opens generously to the southern view, yet is shielded from the sun's rays by a colonnade. The copper-clad wood-framed roof lifts upward in alar celebration.

The pottery studio and winter garden are satellites to the main house. Their orbit is marked by segments of the water elements, implying another circle around the knoll. The pottery studio is nested into the trees to the west, and the winter garden sits on open terraced gardens to the east. The pottery studio is private, and the winter garden is revealed through a slice of the growth to the paths below.

The Sculpture Garden

The sculpture garden is conceived as a sculpture walk, which encircles the hill, providing the route for a variety of settings for sculpture. The sculpture walk facilitates the desire to walk around the hill and experience it as sculpture. This walk occurs at plinth level, and is demarcated by a row of sycamore trees, which runs along the oval contour, making a level line marking out the skirt.

The terraces at the center of the winery connect the building to the hill and introduce the visitor to the sculpture garden. The broad terraces to the east are shaded areas with walks and benches to view individually sited sculpture.

The sculpture walk that encircles the hill provides a structure for the location of sculpture both present and future. In the northern sector the walk connects to terraces that descend to a small walled garden in the corner of the site. The sculpture walk's round form reiterates the circular forms of the house and winery.

The triangular clearing and the vineyard below are canvases for works to be seen from afar. The water element in the clearing is visible from the highway, while the aeration ponds are paintings to be viewed from the tasting room and residence.

Elevations: Residence, Winter Garden, and Pottery Shed, 1984
ink and airbrush on vellum
30 x 40″ (76.2 x 101.6)

Water Elements

The form of the courtyard pools and waterfall completes the geometrics of the house. The broad curve of the waterfall over polished granite creates a light-reflecting band visible from the road below.

On the cleared southern face of the winery hill, the form of the upper waterfall is repeated. This is one portion of a segmented work encircling the knoll at midsection.

On the east and west slopes of the knoll (near the winter garden and pottery studio respectively), the encircling segments are also stone and water pieces but of a different nature. Enclosed in the scrub forest, they are more rustic and textured and would be more intimately experienced. By their length and form, they describe the changing natural topography of the knoll.

The aeration pond in the vineyard—a circle embraced by a square—coordinates with the overall generative geometric plan of the project. With the intended expansion of the winery operations, the area now inside the low berm walls would become the necessary second aeration pond.

Stanley Saitowitz

Toby Levy

Pat O'Brien

Elyn Zimmerman

Stanley Saitowitz was born in Johannesburg, South Africa, in 1948. He received his architectural training at the University of Witwatersrand, Johannesburg, South Africa (B. Arch., 1974), and the University of California, Berkeley (M. Arch., 1977), where he has taught since 1979. His design projects include the Transvaal Residence, Halfway House Estate, South Africa (1978), and the Sundial House in Palimino Lakes, California (1980), where the organization of vertical shadows and colors are attuned to the time of day and season. He is also known for the design of the Wurster Hall auditorium at the University of California, Berkeley (1982), and two California wineries, the Storybook Winery (partially built) in Calistoga (1982) and the Quady Winery in Madera (1983). Saitowitz was recognized for his winning design for the Sukkah Competition, sponsored by the Jewish Community Museum in San Francisco (1984). Saitowitz's work has been exhibited in New York, San Francisco, Rome, Seattle, and Los Angeles. His work was included in the exhibition *California Counterpoint: Architecture 1982*, organized by the Institute for Architecture and Urban Studies, New York, and the San Francisco Art Institute (travelled, catalog published), and in a one-person exhibition at the Matrix Gallery, University Art Museum, University of California, Berkeley, 1985.

He currently resides in San Francisco.

Selected Bibliography
California Counterpoint: Architecture 1982. New York: Institute for Architecture and Urban Studies and Rizzoli, 1982.
Giovannini, Joseph. "Bold Imaginings: 10 California Architects." *New York Times*, 14 July 1983: C1, C10.
Miller, Nory. "Calculated Uncertainty." *Progressive Architecture* 63 (March 1982): 86-91.
The Sukkah Competition. San Francisco: Jewish Community Museum, 1984.

Toby Levy was born in New York in 1951. She was educated at Columbia University, New York (B.A. 1972), and the University of California, Berkeley, where she received her Master of Architecture degree in 1975. Levy has had her own practice, Toby S. Levy, AIA & Associates, in San Francisco since 1978. In 1981, she received the Women in Design International Competition award for her design of the Gianni Versace boutiques (1982) in San Francisco's Crocker Galleria.

Levy's recent projects include the Cornucopia Restaurant in San Francisco (1984); the South Park Renovation in downtown San Francisco for residential and commerical use (1984); and a proposal for the Sukkah Competition sponsored by the Jewish Community Museum, San Francisco (1984). She has been a visiting lecturer at Columbia University, New York (1984).

She currently resides in San Francisco.

Selected Bibliography
Arts and Architecture 3 (1984): 50.
"Small Spaces, Urban and Suburban Refinements." *Archetype* 2 (Autumn 1980): 9, 13.
The Sukkah Competition. San Francisco: Jewish Community Museum, 1984.
"View Wall and Corner Hearth for the Family Room." *Sunset Magazine* 168 (May 1982): 168.

Pat O'Brien was born in 1946 in Dayton, Ohio. She was educated at Pitzer College, Claremont, California (1964-66), and the University of California, Berkeley (B.A. 1968), where she received her Master of Landscape Architecture degree in 1975. Upon graduation, O'Brien worked for SWA Group (formerly Sasaki Walker Associates) in Sausalito, California, and EDAW, Inc., in San Francisco. O'Brien is presently a principal in the San Francisco firm of Meacham O'Brien Landscape Architects which she established in 1978. The firm's projects include the San Francisco International Airport South Terminal and the Life Sciences Center, Library, and Arts Center at Mills College, Oakland. She has worked on community facilities, commercial, educational, and residential projects, and participated in the historic restoration of the Filoli estate gardens in Redwood City, California (1975). O'Brien was a visiting lecturer at the University of California, Berkeley, from 1981 to 1984 and is the author of *Filoli: The Design of the Gardens* (1976 and 1977) and *Plants for California Landscapes: A Catalogue of Drought Tolerant Plants* (1979) produced for the California Department of Water Resources.

She currently resides in San Francisco.

Elyn Zimmerman was born in Philadelphia in 1945. She studied at the University of California, Los Angeles (B.A., 1968, M.F.A., 1972). Her work was included in the 1980 Venice Biennale and has been the subject of numerous one-person exhibitions at institutions including the University Art Museum, University of California, Berkeley, 1974; the Museum of Contemporary Art, Chicago, 1979 (catalog published); and the Hudson River Museum, Yonkers, New York, 1982 (catalog published). She has received several National Endowment for the Arts grants including an exchange fellowship which enabled her to visit Japan in 1981. Recognized for her site-specific sculpture, Zimmerman's major projects include *Sightline/Access*, which she designed for the 1980 Winter Olympics at Lake Placid, New York. She recently completed *Marabar* for the headquarters of the National Geographic Society in Washington, D.C., and is presently installing a commissioned sculpture and environs for the Dade County Courthouse, Miami, Florida.

She currently resides in New York.

Selected Bibliography
Donohue, Marlena. "The Galleries." *Los Angeles Times*, 19 October 1984: 13.
Garris, Laurie. "The Changing Landscape." *Arts and Architecture* 3 (1984): 56-59.
Gopnik, Adam. "Marabar." *Arts Magazine* 59 (October 1984): 78-79.
Lyons, Lisa. "Eight Artists: The Elusive Image." *Design Quarterly* 111/112. Minneapolis: Walker Art Center, 1979.
Varnedoe, Kirk. "Site Lines: Recent Work by Elyn Zimmerman." *Arts Magazine* 53 (December 1978): 148-151.

Team Members
Architects
Daniel Solomon
Ricardo Bofill
Patrick Dillon
Artist
Ed Carpenter
Landscape Architect
Barbara Stauffacher Solomon
Drawings
Connie Giles
Kent Macdonald
Laura Nettleton
Models
Thomas Cowen
Matthius DeBoer
Suzanne Taj-Eldin
Lyanne Sueuga

Introduction:

The site for Clos Pegase contains an absolute and frail duality–
volcanic knob and alluvial plain, wild nature, and rational fur-
rows. The competition program describes a winery ⅓ the girth
of the knob and ⅕ its height. A large building at the base of the
hill would eradicate the sharp and delicate geometry which is
the site's special virtue. Our winery, therefore, stands away
from the hill and joins with it to shape a vineyard which is both
a monumental public square and a continuation of the valley
floor. The almost perfect order of the hill is gently corrected–its
base made circular and distinct with a giant bench. The hill and
its forest are split (by the hoof of enraged Pegasus); water spills
forth in a red channel that springs from the center of the hilltop
residence and flows to the winery in the valley floor. The red
channel is visible from Highway 29 and marks Clos Pegase.

Elements / From South to North:

Parking in an orchard / Ponds traversed by bridges to the winery / Columns standing in the ponds enclosing water rooms /
Cacti growing from the columns / The winery reflected in water /
Ramps ascending to a rooftop sculpture garden / A walnut
alleé and tall palms making the vineyard into a great square /
The square bisected by a red water channel and paths / Large
sculpture in the vineyard along the path / The bench marking
the edge of hill and valley / Winding paths through woods /
Water descending from a great door / The house around a
courtyard / Terraces for various pleasures.

The Winery:

The winery is organized around two major spaces: a tall central
room extending like a nave north and south through the building, and a two-level street for forklifts below and public circulation above. Both major spaces are marked by glass roofs
fabricated by the collaborating artist.

Public rooms, administration, central wine-making functions,
and service spaces are organized on two levels around the major
central room. The two-level streets extend east and west from
the central room. To the north of the streets are the large phase

Model, 1984
plaster, pigment, polystyrene, steel wool, foam, nails, and cork
9¼ x 27 x 60″ (23.5 x 68.6 x 152.4)

Patrick Dillon
Site Plan, 1984
ink and colored pencil on vellum
40 x 30″ (101.6 x 76.2)

one functions: barrel and tank storage, cased goods, and bottle storage. South of the streets are the phase two expansion spaces. The street itself will be an exterior arcade at phase one.

The phasing and expansion are configured so that all public outdoor spaces and the main views of the winery are complete at phase one. The view of the winery and its service areas from the residence, and use of the winery gardens as extensions of the private gardens, were considerations influencing the placement of the winery. At the end of the streets are the truck-receiving porches and trellised porches into which the ponds extend.

Circulation / Cars and Trucks:
Visitors and staff enter the south end of the site, park south of the ponds, and cross bridges to the winery.

Trucks serving bottle and cased goods storage enter the site north of the winery and use the public road to exit in a continuous forward loop.

Trucks serving the grape receiving and crushing area use a turf-block frontage road along Dunaweal Lane. The receiving of the grapes is festive and ceremonial. This function is housed in a trellised porch on the public side of the building.

Public:
Tours begin at the reception area, visit the central functions along the main room, ascend the stairs to galleries above, and proceed down bridges over the interior streets.

Forklifts:
The central interior street serves forklifts and links all functions in the winery. Forklifts have access to the bottling and processing areas from the wood barrel storage room and from the central public room. Similarly, the shop and lab areas across the public room have access from two sides.

Other Circulation:
The kitchen is served from the forklift by elevator and dumbwaiter.

71

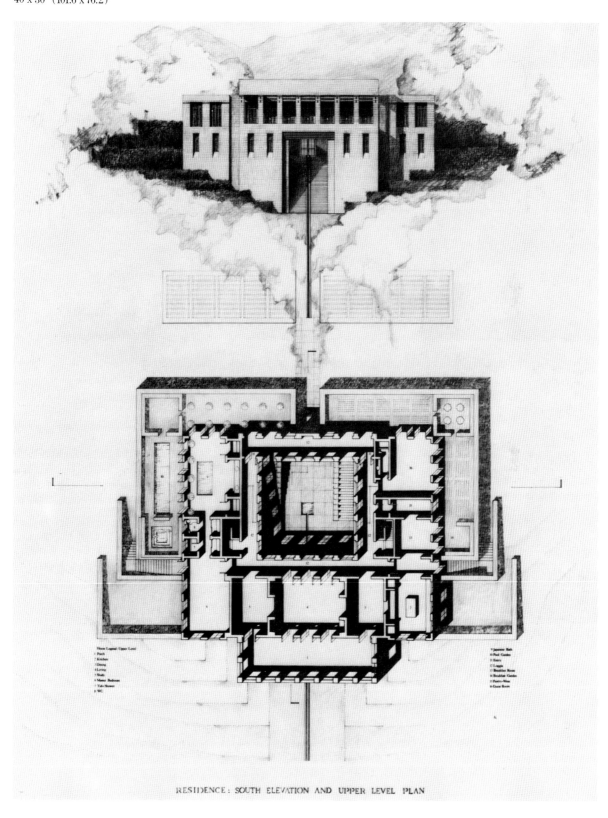

RESIDENCE: SOUTH ELEVATION AND UPPER LEVEL PLAN

Dining in the rooftop sculpture garden is served by dumbwaiter.
Handicapped access to upper levels is by elevator.
Gardening equipment is brought to the roof by elevator.

Art in the Winery:
At numerous locations along public routes through the winery there are expansive areas of wall for the display of art. These include the entry foyers, the center of the main public room, open rooms at the top of the stairs to the second level, and walls along the second level galleries.

The upper level bridges over the forklift street are part of the main public tour route through the winery. The eastern bridge is completely open to the working winery below. The western bridge is partially enclosed by walls displaying art with occasional glimpses through openings into the large storage areas.

Sculpture:
There are three sculpture gardens—the formal roof garden, the vineyard square, and the romantic natural garden on the lower hillside. Access to all the sculpture areas is through the winery; the ramps to the winery roof, the vineyard, and woods are secured from public access by a ha-ha or trench along the road and concealed fencing in the woods.

The formal roof garden gives the land of the winery back to the valley, particularly as viewed from above. The roof is a vineyard. Walking through this vineyard one passes through green rooms of clipped juniper hedge in which sculpture is placed. At the center is a dining terrace overlooking a pool which terminates the red channel of Pegasus that begins on the hillside.

A few large sculptures are located along the axis of the red channel. The path provides a rare instance of public access to a working vineyard.

Where the red channel intersects the bench at the base of the hill, meandering paths lead right and left to small clearings in the woods which are locations for sculptures as well as a small public amphitheater.

Barbara Stauffacher Solomon
Winery: Sculpture Garden, 1984
colored pencil on vellum
30 x 40″ (76.2 x 101.6)

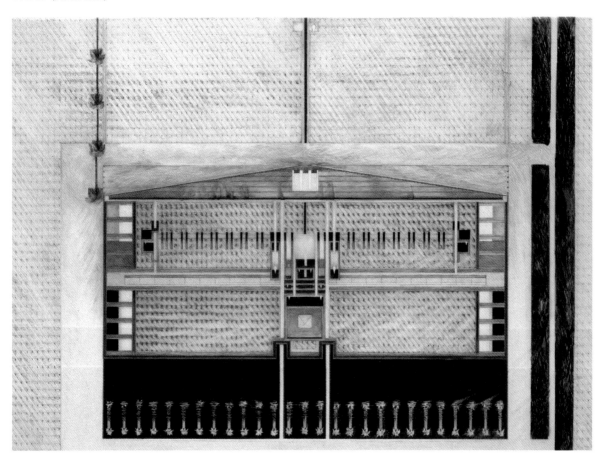

Ed Carpenter
Drawing for Leaded Glass Skylight (detail), 1984
ink and colored pencil on paper
10½ x 167 x 2½″ (26.8 x 424.2 x 6.4)

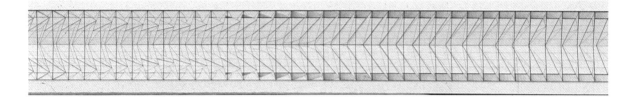

Color and Material:

The winery program suggests a large, simple building with little fenestration. The color and quality of its surfaces are therefore critical. Throughout the vicinity there are volcanic soils which are characterized by the strong reddish tonalities of iron oxide. These red earth tones are our palette for both the winery and the residence.

The material for both buildings is block manufactured by the existing technology for concrete block. Variations in the mixing, curing, and surfacing processes, manipulation of aggregate composition, and addition of mineral and oxide pigments transform this basic material. Hues range from the warm yellow side to the cool violet side of red. These are the colors of vineyard leaves in autumn.

Other cement and gypsum-based materials for both the residence and winery, such as interior plaster and precast elements, will be manipulated to blend or contrast with the blocks.

Other materials are as follows:

Winery
Floors: slab on grade; unglazed ceramic tile at public areas; perforated steel sheet on bridges.

Interior walls
Block and skim coat gypsum plaster with internal tint.

Roof
Elastometric membrane with two feet of soil.

Residence
Exterior walls: block as above with smooth ground surface.

Interior walls: gypsum plaster.

Floors: unglazed ceramic tile.

Roof structure: timber.

The Residence:
The residence is a classical villa around a courtyard. Guests arrive at the hilltop and park under a pergola at the lower level of the house. Residents park in garages and enter the courtyard at the front gate. From this entry there is a view south through a giant portal to the valley and winery below. A monumental stair descends through the portal and leads laterally to smaller stairs through the woods to the valley floor. These stairs will have security fences and gates concealed in the woods.

The lower level contains children's rooms and the pottery studio opening onto outdoor terraces. In the center of the court is a small pool, the source of the red channel that runs through Clos Pegase. From the court, stairs lead up to entry doors and a loggia surrounding the court for the display of art. Main rooms and a trellised porch face south to the sun and view. East and west extensions of the loggia lead down to lower terraces and flower gardens. The breakfast and guest rooms open directly onto an east garden for cultivation of herbs and vegetables and outdoor dining. The Japanese bath and pool garden face the west and north views of Mount St. Helena and the northern ridge. Rows of french doors linking indoor spaces to gardens and layering delicate patterns over the garden views will be fabricated by the collaborating artist.

Across the entry court and through the pergola a small stair leads to a north-facing terrace and a special view at early evening.

Collaboration:
In the classical world, buildings and landscapes were crafted and rational. Rule governed circumstance. The inherent rationality of architecture was derived from an analysis of its elements. Combination and recombination of elements acquired from past experience were the basis of invention. Rule provided the points of connection for the works of farmers, gardeners, artisans of all sorts, and the architect. Distinctions between artist and artisan, artisan and architect, architect and gardener, gardener and urbanist were blurred. This blurred vision was a vision of paradise which motivated earthly pursuits for centuries. Clos Pegase is about paradise.

75

Daniel Solomon

Barbara Stauffacher Solomon

Daniel Solomon was born in San Francisco in 1939. He was educated at Stanford University, California (B.A., 1962); Columbia University, New York (B. Arch., 1963); and the University of California, Berkeley (M. Arch., 1966). Since 1967, he has taught at the University of California, Berkeley, and is the principal of the firm of Daniel Solomon and Associates, San Francisco, which he established the same year. Recognized as an influential educator and urban planner, he received a *Progressive Architecture* Urban Design award in 1979 for "Change Without Loss," a study on residential areas in San Francisco which resulted in a change in the city's zoning code. Known for multiple-scale residential work, his recent San Francisco projects include a variation on the traditional San Francisco Victorians, the Glover Street Condominiums (1981), and the Amancio Ergina Village providing low and moderate income housing. He has recently completed the partial renovation of the San Francisco Public Library, and is presently working on planning studies for the city of Oakland on downtown redevelopment and on residential zoning for the city of San Jose, California. A Fellow of the American Institute of Architects, he has lectured extensively in this country and abroad. Solomon's work was included in *The California Condition*, 1982, curated by Stanley Tigerman and Susan Grant Lewin for the La Jolla Museum of Contemporary Art, California (catalog published), and he was among eight West Coast architects chosen to participate in the 1983 Chicago World's Fair Design Charette held at the University of California, Los Angeles.

He currently resides in San Francisco.

Selected Bibliography
The California Condition. La Jolla, Ca.: La Jolla Museum of Contemporary Art, 1982.
Ketchum, Diana. "San Francisco in Context." *Arts and Architecture* 3 (1984): 37, 56.
Oliver, Richard, ed. *The Making of an Architect, 1881-1981.* New York: Rizzoli, 1981.
"The 26th P/A Awards." *Progressive Architecture* 60 (January 1979): 106.

Barbara Stauffacher Solomon, a native San Franciscan, attended the California School of Fine Arts (now the San Francisco Art Institute), studied graphic design at the Allgemeine Gewerbeschule, Kunstgewerbliche Abteilungen, Schule für Gestaltung Vogelsangstr in Basel, Switzerland (1959-61), and graduated from the University of California, Berkeley (B.A., 1977, M. Arch., 1981). Stauffacher Solomon's work continually enhances architecture by linking it to related disciplines including graphic design and landscape architecture. In 1970, she was awarded the Industrial Arts medal by the American Institute of Architects for Supergraphics, which utilizes primary colors and elementary shapes to enhance architectural structures. Among the first projects to incorporate Stauffacher Solomon's design concepts was MLTW/Turnbull Associates, San Francisco, for *Sea Ranch* (1966) in Sea Ranch, California, for which she was honored by the American Institute of Architects in 1967 and 1968. Currently, she is concerned with developing and maintaining green spaces in urban and rural environments. She has collaborated with Taller de Arquitectura on El Jardin del Turia (1982) in Valencia, Spain, and her concepts were the subject of the exhibition *Green Architecture: Notes on the Common Ground*, 1982, organized by the Walker Art Center, Minneapolis (travelled, catalog published). Among the exhibitions featuring her work are *The California Condition*, 1982 organized by the La Jolla Museum of Contemporary Art, California, and *High Styles: Twentieth-Century American Design* organized by the Whitney Museum of American Art, New York, to open in November 1985. Stauffacher Solomon has been a visiting lecturer at institutions including the University of California, Berkeley; Yale University, New Haven, Connecticut; and, in 1983, she was a Fellow at the American Academy in Rome.

She currently resides in San Francisco.

Selected Bibliography
Bissell, Terry, Goldstein, Barbara, and Perrin, Deborah. "Plotting the Land." *Arts and Architecture* 1 (1983): 45-53.
Dietz, Paula. "A Cultivated Civilization." *Metropolis* 3 (March 1984): 14-17, 30-31.
"Green Architecture: Notes on the Common Ground." *Design Quarterly 120*. Minneapolis: Walker Art Center, 1982.
Meggs, Philip. *The History of Graphic Design.* New York: Van Nostrand Reinhold, 1983.

Ricardo Bofill

Patrick Dillon

Ed Carpenter

Ricardo Bofill was born in Barcelona, Spain, in 1939. He received his training at the Escuela Tecnica Superior de Arquitectura de Barcelona, Spain (1955-56), and the School of Architecture of Geneva (1957-60). In 1963, he established the architectural studio Taller de Arquitectura in Barcelona, Spain. In its first period, the team concentrated on recovering crafted elements of traditional Catalan architecture, culminating in the construction of *Barrio Gaudi* (1968) in Tarragona, Spain. Subsequently, they developed a methodology based on the geometric formation of elements in space, as demonstrated in the building of *Walden 7* (1975) in Barcelona. In 1971, Bofill formed a complementary team in Paris to work on the development of French *New Towns*. The Taller worked in Algeria on several government projects in 1978. Since 1979, the Taller de Arquitectura simultaneously developed four projects in Versailles, Marne-la-Vallee, Paris, and Montpellier, France. Presently the Taller is working on prefabricated housing in France and the renewal of suburban areas with proposals for green spaces in Spain. Bofill's work, along with that of Leon Krier, is the subject of an exhibition organized by The Museum of Modern Art, New York, scheduled to open in June 1985.

He currently resides in Barcelona, Spain.

Selected Bibliography
Bergdoll, B. "Subsidized Doric [Spaces of Abraxas, Marne-la-Vallee, France]. *Progressive Architecture* 63 (October 1982): 74-79.
Frampton, K. "Prospects for a Critical Regionalism." *Perspecta* 20: 150.
Glancy, J. "Factory Conversion, Barcelona." *Architectural Record* 174 (November 1983): 74-78.
Hodgkinson, P. "Gardens in Spain." *Progressive Architecture* 65 (June 1984): 88-93.
Ricardo Bofill, Taller de Arquitectura. Barcelona, Spain: Editorial Gustavo Gili, S.A., 1984.

Patrick Dillon was born in Antón, Panama, in 1952. He was educated at Rollins College, Winter Park, Florida; Arizona State University, Tempe (B. Arch., 1976); and Rice University, Houston (M. Arch., 1978). During 1976 to 1977 he worked in Houston for the Department of Traffic Planning and for 3D International, an architectural engineering firm. In 1978 he joined Taller de Arquitectura where he assisted on major projects for the firm including Les Espaces de Abraxas (1979) in Marne-la-Vallee, France; Antigonia (1980) in Montpellier, France; El Jardin del Turia (1981) in Valencia, Spain; and Villiage E and F (1979) in Bechar, Algeria. Since 1984 he has been the Design Director of Taller de Arquitectura in Paris where his projects include the Times Square Competition, New York (1984); the Hotel Royal Apartments (1984), a resort on the Breton coast in La Baule, France; and an urban design for Creteil New Town, France (1984).

He currently resides in Paris.

Ed Carpenter was born in Los Angeles in 1946. He attended the University of California, Santa Barbara (1965-66), and Berkeley (1968-70). An architectural glass designer, Carpenter began working with glass in 1971. In 1973, he studied stained glass design and technique with Patrick Reyntiens in Buckinghamshire, England, and received the Michael Hattrell Award for the study of stained glass in modern architecture from the Burleighfield Association, also in Buckinghamshire. In 1975 Carpenter studied large architectural stained glass design with Ludwig Schaffrath in Alsdorf, West Germany, on a grant from the Graham Foundation for Advanced Study in the Fine Arts. His design projects include the Justice Center, Portland, Oregon (1983); the skylight for the Security Life Building, Denver (1983); and the Performing Arts Center in Eugene, Oregon (1981). He is currently at work on a commission for the First Community Church in Dallas. He is the recipient of several National Endowment for the Arts grants and a Western States Arts Foundation Fellowship. In 1981, he was invited to New Zealand by their Glass Artists Society to teach and lecture. From 1975 to 1979 he served as Chairman of the Building Committee at the Oregon School of Arts and Crafts in Portland during the planning for the construction of a new campus. He is Chairman of the Board of Directors of the American Craft Enterprises, New Paltz, New York, and serves on the board of the American Craft Council, New York.

He currently resides in Portland, Oregon.

Selected Bibliography
Brenner, Douglas. "Justice Center, Portland, Oregon." *Architectural Record* 172 (June 1984):126-135.
Clarke, Brian, ed. *Architectural Stained Glass.* London: John Murray, 1979.
Curtiss, Terry. "The Art of Architectural Glass." *Architecture California* 6 (May/June 1984): 31-33.
Poensgen, Jochem. "Light-Farbe-Glas." *Neues Glas* 2 (1983): 68-73
Rigon, Otto. *New Glass.* San Francisco: San Francisco Book Company, 1976.

The Award of the Jury:
Graves/Schmidt

Team Members

Design Team
Michael Graves, Project Architect
Edward Schmidt, Project Artist
Juliet Richardson-Smith, Designer
Terence Smith, Designer
Susan Butcher, Assistant
Alexey Grigorieff, Assistant
Ronald Berlin, Assistant
Mehrdad Yazdani, Assistant

Presentation Team
Raymond Beeler
Ronald Berlin
Theodore Brown
Patrick Burke
Jesse Castañeda
Albert Chini
David Coleman
Michael Crackel
David Dymecki
Cheryl Ginenthal
Nicholas Gonser
Thomas Hanrahan
Lynda Kilburn
Michael Kuhling
Gary Lapera
Robert Marino
Leslie Mason
Victoria Meyers
Peter Neilson
James Pricco
Eric Regh
Anita Rosskam
Thomas Rowe
Keat Tan
Peter Twombly
Lesley Wellman
Karen Wheeler

Model Team
Alex Lee, Model Maker
Jane Vogel, Colorist
Douglass Paschall, Assistant
Donald Strum, Assistant
Keat Tan
Jesse Castañeda
Megan Downer
Lynda Kilburn
Peter Neilson
Sharon Pachter
Debra O'Brien
Anita Rosskam
Suzanne Strum
William Taylor

The myth of Pegasus tells us that the hoofprints struck by
the winged horse landing on Mount Helikon were the beginning
of the spring of the Muses, the founding of the arts. The waters
of the spring can be seen as providing both spiritual and physical
sustenance, as the arts inspire our imagination and the waters
irrigate our fields. It is fitting that Dionysus, god of wine, was
the favorite pupil of the Muses, for also within the art of wine
making, there exists the duality of the process of making the
wine and the pleasure of drinking it. Within this larger context,
we have developed the themes of wine making, the cycles of the
day and the seasons, and the relationship of the man-made to
the natural landscape.

The site of the Clos Pegase winery has been organized along an
axis of water beginning with the spring, the grotto of Pegasus,
carved into the summit of the knoll, and ending in the natural
landscape at the winery's ponds. To one side of this axis are the
public activities of the winery and the sculpture garden, and,
to the other side, are the wine-making functions. The residence,
located on the "private" side of the axis, is protected from the
public and production activities and enjoys views of the vineyards
to the south and east.

The visitor approaches the complex through a large public
forecourt oriented to Route 29. A sculpture of Pegasus is placed
above the main portico as a symbol of the winery. The main
winery building is divided into two sections symmetrically dis-
posed about an open-air portico. Though different in use, these
two parts have been given a unified public image, thereby collecting into the street facade the dual aspects of wine making,
process and pleasure. To the east of the entry portico is the
winery itself, with its various processing and storage facilities.
An outdoor working court, accessible for service from Dunaweal Lane, is separated from the public vehicular entrance to
the complex. The west half of the winery building holds rooms
for tastings and other public functions. The visitor entering the
portico is greeted by a receptionist and is either escorted on
a tour of the winery to the right, directed to the tasting rooms
to the left, or allowed to enter the sculpture park and gardens.

The procession through the sculpture gardens begins at a circular building, stepped in section, which is seen as a symbolic mountain, the mountain of Pegasus. This building would be used for visitor orientation and also as a gathering place for parties and outdoor wine tastings. In location and character, the building stands between the natural landscape of the knoll and vineyards, and the other buildings of the winery. As garden architecture, it embodies and makes public the several dual themes of the project: landscape and building, work and pleasure. The interior of this round symbolic mountain is banded by a continuous frieze depicting the cycle of the wine-making process through the seasons of the year, from planting, to harvesting, to wine making, and to the drinking and enjoyment of wine. The narrative, told both in the building and in the medium of painting, is intriguing in its appeal not only to our visual senses, but also to our intellectual, storytelling interests.

The sculpture park is designed to provide a series of different places or landscapes for the exhibition of sculpture. The journey through the park leads from a man-made landscape to a more romantic and natural one, and is organized by a continuous path beginning and ending at the symbolic mountain. The first large significant place within the sculpture park is a flat lawn or terrace, carved into the hillside. Sculpture is set into niches in a wall of green, and is seen frontally against that wall. From the terrace, the visitor enters a free open meadow–untamed nature –where sculpture is seen in the round within the landscape. A small garden theater is located on the edge of this meadow, providing a natural setting for theater and concerts as well as a "stage" for the placement of sculpture.

The visitor then takes a winding, tree-lined scissor path which climbs up the natural hillside, and gives views of sculpture from a variety of vantage points. The path culminates in the grotto of Pegasus within the summit of the knoll. From the grotto's terrace, one views the vineyards to the south and east, the path by which one came, and the water course which is the axis dividing the two sides of the site. One then proceeds down a water stair, across an aqueduct carrying water to the symbolic mountain

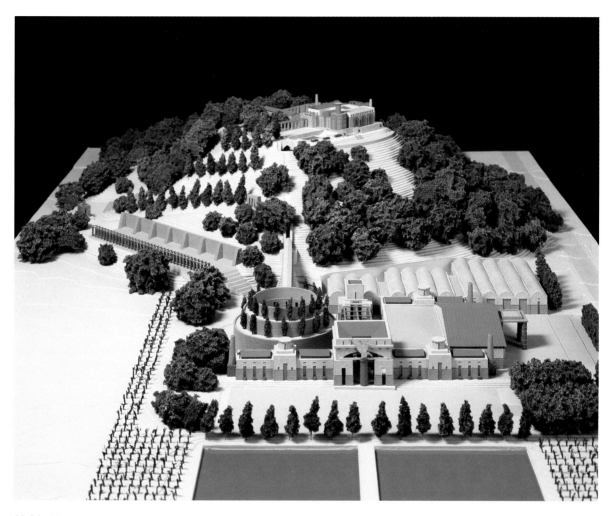

Model, 1984
cardboard, paper, paint, sponge, and wood
7¹/₂ x 27¹/₂ x 58¹/₂″ (19.1 x 69.9 x 148.6)

Site Plan, 1984
ink and colored pencil on paper
30 x 40″ (76.2 x 101.6)

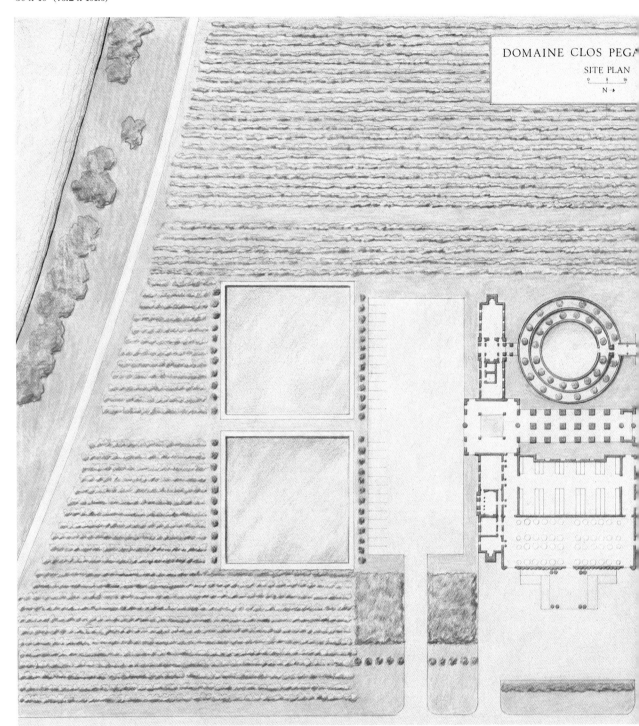

DOMAINE CLOS PEGA

SITE PLAN

0   8   16

N →

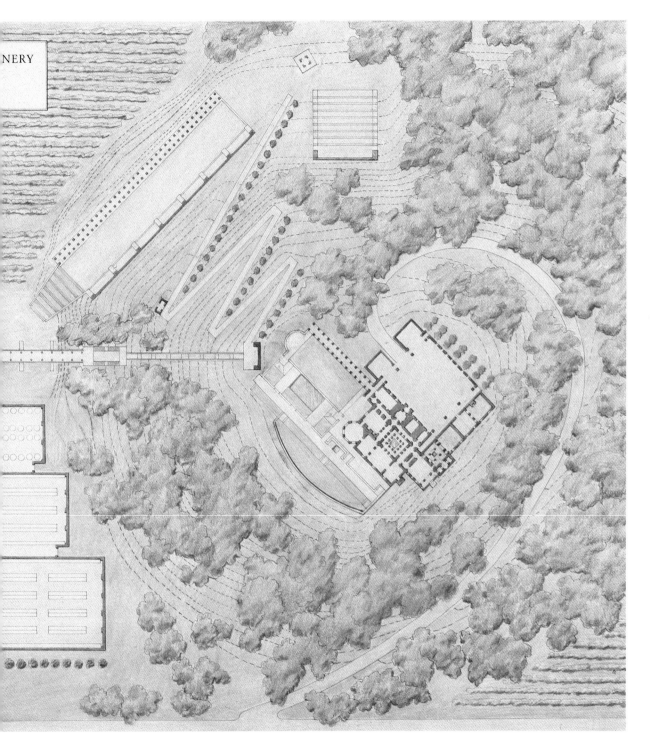

Edward Schmidt
Untitled, 1984
oil on canvas
two friezes,
each 7½ x 55″
(19.1 x 139.7) (sight)

and vineyards below, and finally arrives at the top of the mountain which one descends by an outdoor, planted stair encircling
the building. The water course provides orientation within the
site and also contributes to the thematic story being told. The
aqueduct, a man-made artifact which "tames" and directs the
water for irrigation and our physical sustenance, is designed
as a rustic bridge set between the more romantic natural landscape of the knoll above and the replica of the mountain below.

The house is located at the top of the natural hillside within
its own private precinct which is connected yet distinct from the
public sculpture park. Organized around a central atrium, the
major areas of the house are oriented primarily to the south
and west. The private wing, however, including master bedroom,
Japanese bath, and pottery studio, is seen as a series of pavilions
pulled away from the main living spaces and is oriented with
a view of the Clos Pegase vineyards to the east.

The main living spaces of the house look to the south, toward
the vineyards, past a sweeping outdoor terrace and lawn. The
dining room is organized with its own formal terrace, overlook-

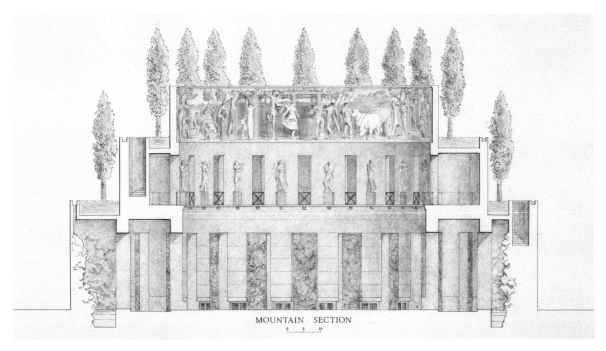

MOUNTAIN SECTION

0   8   16

Office of Michael Graves with Edward Schmidt
Mountain Section, 1984
ink and colored pencil on paper
10 x 18″ (25.4 x 45.7)

ing an outdoor court to the west planted with flower and vegetable gardens. A two-story octagonal winter garden provides
a circulation hinge between the living room and dining room as
well as a focal point for the organization of the exterior gardens.
A private path leads from the lawn to the grotto of Pegasus from
where one descends on foot to the winery along the water course.

A variety of architectural styles or characters may be found
within Napa Valley, and our scheme for the Clos Pegase winery
tends to evoke memories of a European ancestry. Character has
been suggested by our attempt to establish a more archaic or
timeless sensibility. Within the narrative or esthetic text of this setting, the stories of wine making and habitation can best be told.

We have assumed that the work of the collaborating artist on this
project should not be in competition with the client's art collection.
We have therefore attempted to establish the collaboration by the
traditional reinforcement of art with architecture and architecture with art. This is achieved, we feel, by the identification
of the text and narrative within the surfaces of the architecture
itself. In addition to the painted surfaces, three-dimensional
artifacts have also been proposed. These artifacts or figures are
similar to the paintings in that they are seen as embellishments
to the collaborative text and to the architecture itself.

Michael Graves
Winery Entry Portico Study, 1984
graphite on tracing paper
9¾ x 9″ (24.8 x 22.9)

Michael Graves
Residence: South Elevation, 1984
graphite and colored pencil on tracing paper
10⅛ x 16¼″ (25.7 x 41.3)

Michael Graves
South Elevation, 1984
ink, gouache, and colored pencil
on paper mounted on board
30 x 40″ (76.2 x 101.6)

Michael Graves was born in Indianapolis in 1934. He received his architectural training at the University of Cincinnati (B. Arch., 1958) and Harvard University, Cambridge, Massachusetts (M. Arch., 1959). He was awarded the Prix de Rome in 1960 and studied at the American Academy in Rome, of which he is now Trustee and President of the Society of Fellows. Graves is Schirmer Professor of Architecture at Princeton University, New Jersey, where he has taught since 1962. While his early work was primarily residential, Graves's firm, Michael Graves, Architect, is recognized for corporate commissions and recently designed The Portland Building, Oregon (1980); the Sunar Furniture Showroom, New York (1981); the Humana Corporate Headquarters Building, Louisville, Kentucky (1982); the San Juan Capistrano Public Library, California (1980); and was a finalist in the Ohio University Visual Arts Center competition, Columbus (1983). He is the architect for the expansions of the Whitney Museum of American Art, New York (1981), as well as the Newark Museum, New Jersey (1982), which he originally designed (1968). A fellow of the American Institute of Architects, Graves has won eleven *Progressive Architecture* design awards, three National American Institute of Architects honor awards, and, in 1980, the American Academy and Institute of Arts and Letters awarded him the Arnold W. Brunner Memorial Prize in Architecture. He is a recognized designer of interiors and furniture and a painter. Graves has designed furniture for the Memphis Collection, and was included in a group of eleven internationally renowned architects commissioned by Alessi Fratelli, the Italian housewares firm, to design silver tea and coffee services which formed the travelling exhibition *Architecture in Silver*, 1980, organized by the Max Protetch Gallery, New York (catalog published). The numerous exhibitions featuring Graves's work include the 1980 Venice Biennale; *Buildings for Best Products*, 1979, The Museum of Modern Art, New York; and *Architecture and Art*, 1983, the Museum of Contemporary Art, Montreal.

He currently resides in Princeton, New Jersey.

90

Michael Graves

Selected Bibliography
Arnell, Peter, Bickford, Ted, and Wheeler, Karen Vogel, ed. *Michael Graves: Projects 1966-1981.* New York: Rizzoli, 1983.
Drexler, Arthur. *Transformations in Modern Architecture.* New York: The Museum of Modern Art, 1980.
Eisenman, Peter. "The Graves of Modernism." *Oppositions* 12 (Spring 1978, published 1979).
Guenther, Robert. "Newer than New? In Architect's Circles, Post-Modern Design Is a Bone of Contention." *Wall Street Journal*, 1 August 1983: 1, 12.
Jencks, Charles. *Kings of Infinite Space: Michael Graves and Frank Lloyd Wright.* London: St. Martin's Press, 1984.

Edward Schmidt

Edward Schmidt was born in Ann Arbor, Michigan, in 1946. He studied at the Pratt Institute, Brooklyn (B.F.A., 1971); the École des Beaux Arts, Paris; and Brooklyn College, City University of New York (M.F.A., 1974). Since 1974, he has taught painting at a number of institutions including the New York Academy of Art (1982, 1984) and the Art Students League, New York (1984). In 1983, Schmidt was awarded the Prix de Rome by the American Academy in Rome and received an artist grant from the Ingram Merrill Foundation, New York, the following year. His first one-person exhibition was held at the Salve Regina Gallery, Catholic University, Washington, D.C., in 1980. Subsequent solo exhibitions include the Bayly Museum of Art, University of Virginia, Charlottesville, 1980, and the Robert Schoelkopf Gallery, New York, 1982. He was recently commissioned to design murals for the Cincinnati Symphony Summer Pavilion (1983) in collaboration with the project architect, Michael Graves, and for the Alwyn Court Landmark Building, New York (1984).

He currently resides in Brooklyn.

Selected Bibliography
Campbell, Lawrence. "Edward Schmidt at Schoelkopf." *Art in America* 71 (February 1983): 132.
Perl, J. "Life of the Object: Still-Life Painting Today." *Arts* 52 (December 1977): 128.
Rosenthal, D. "Metaphor in Painting: The Struggle for a Tradition." *Arts* 52 (June 1978): 140.
Tapley, G.M. "Arcadian Ethos in Contemporary Painting." *Arts* 57 (February 1983): 125.

Goldman/Albuquerque

Ron Goldman
Mitchell Residence, 1982
Malibu, California
Photo: Glen Allison

Lita Albuquerque
Blue Connector, 1978
Malibu, California
Photo: Lita Albuquerque

Jennings & Stout
Schematic Plan: World Savings and Loan,
First Branch, 1983
San Francisco

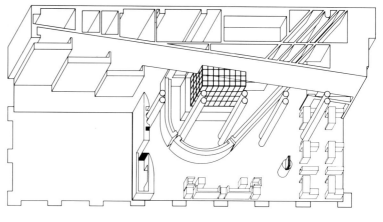

David Bottini
From Memory, 1978
oil pastel and varnish on steel
51 x 26 x 17″ (155 x 66 x 43.2)
Courtesy of Paule Anglim Gallery,
San Francisco
Photo: M. Lee Fatherree

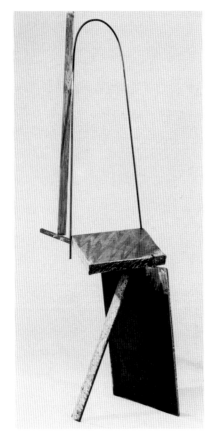

94

Olsen/Walker/Hirshfield

Olsen Walker Architects
Schematic Plan: South Arcade,
Pike Place Market, 1984
Seattle

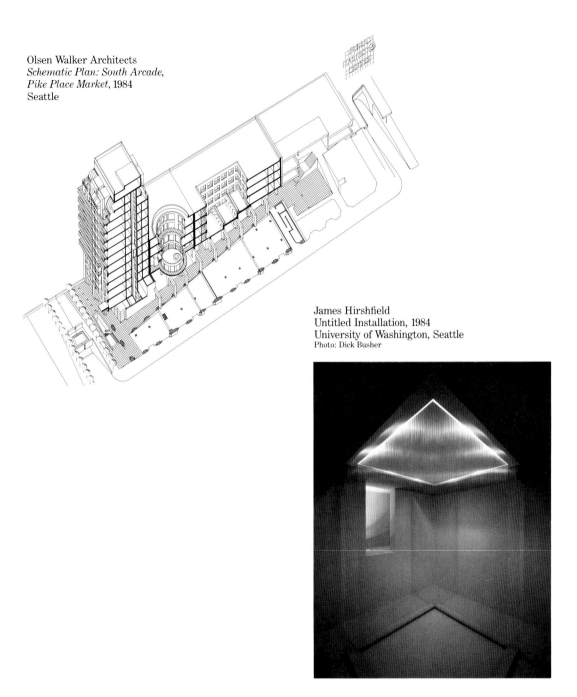

James Hirshfield
Untitled Installation, 1984
University of Washington, Seattle
Photo: Dick Busher

Tom Grondona
A Villa North of San Diego, 1978
Escondido, California
Photo: Tom Grondona

Laddie John Dill
Untitled, 1978
cement polymer and plate glass
72 x 216″ (183 x 548.6)
Courtesy of the artist
Photo: Thomas P. Vinetz

Rob Quigley
Oxley Residence, 1984
La Jolla, California
Photo: John Durant

Ron Wigginton
Starwalk, 1982
Pacific Beach, California
Photo: Nicholas King

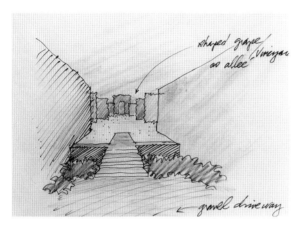

Edgar Haag
Sketch for Schreyer Garden: Grape Topiary, 1983
Photo: Edgar Haag

Moore Lyndon Turnbull Whitaker
Sea Ranch Condominium I, 1965
Sea Ranch, California
Photo: Morley Baer

Douglas Hollis and Richard Turner
A Talking Garden, 1982
The Oakland Museum
Photo: M. Lee Fatherree

The Competition Entries

Architects
Ace Architects
  Lucia Howard
  David Weingarten
Artist
Alan Greenberg
Landscape Architect
William P. Coburn

Architects
ASA Architecture/Planning
  Ross Anderson
  Hildegard Richardson
  Frederic Schwartz
Artist
Mary Miss
Landscape Architect
William Smith

Architects
Backen Arrigoni and
Ross, Inc.
  Howard J. Backen
  Robert V. Arrigoni
  John V. Y. Lee
  Roger Olpin
Artist
Mia Kodani

Architects
Barcelon and Jang
  L. Wayne Barcelon
  Darlene Jang
Artist
Arnaldo Pomodoro

Architects
Batey & Mack
  Andrew Batey
  Mark Mack
Artist
Peter Saari

Architects
Bay Architects and
Associates
  Thomas F. Lee
Artist
Darryl Sapien
Landscape Architect
Donald Ray Carter

Architects
Belli, Christensen
Architects
  Fred Christensen
  Raymond Belli
  Dennis Kennedy
  Lino Belli
Artist
David Ligare

Architects
Berkus Group Architects
  Barry A. Berkus
Artist
Laddie John Dill

Architect
Obie G. Bowman
Artist
Dennis Leon

Architect
Walter Thomas Brooks
Artist
Eric Norstad
Landscape Architect
Satoru Nishita

Architects
Laurance Skylar Brown
and Associates
  Laurance Skylar Brown
Artist
Larry Bell

Architects
Alan Buchsbaum
Michael Sorkin
Artist
Robert Morris

Architects
Callister, Gately and Bischoff
  Charles Warren Callister
  David K. Gately
  James Bischoff
  Joseph O. Newberry
  Michael Heckmann
Artists
Mark Di Suvero
Ralph Funicello
Ruth Zacherle

Architects
Donald Carlson and
Associates
  Donald Carlson
Artist
Lewis "Buster" Simpson

Architects
Carter/Cody Associates
  Virgil R. Carter
  George Cody
  Chris H. Zach
Artist
Keith Boyle

Architect
Lem Chin
Artist
Michael Heinrich

Architects
The Colyer/Freeman Group
  Robert D. Colyer
  S. Pearl Freeman
Artist
Amy Trachtenberg
Landscape Architects
Miller Company
  Jeffrey Miller

Architects
Davis-Centurion-Seuferer
Associates
  Francisco J. Centurion
Artist
Mary Fuller
Landscape Architects
Leffingwell Associates
  Paul Leffingwell

Architects
DiNapoli/Berger Architects
  William DiNapoli
  Miles Berger
Artist
Keith Wilson
Site Designer
Steven Winkel

Architects
Eisenman Robertson
Architects
  Peter Eisenman
Artist
Vito Acconci

Architect
Steven D. Erlich
Artist
Guy Dill

Architects
Massimo Farinelli
Francesca Dei
Aldo Renai
Artist
Robert Ciabani

Architects
Fesckes Associates
  Tibor F. Fesckes
  Andrew T. Fesckes
  Julianna A. Fesckes
Artist
Shari Kadar

Architect
Frederick Fisher
Artist
Eric Orr
Landscape Architect
Keith Ludowitz

Architects
Fitzpatrick/Karren Associates, Architect/AIA, Inc.
  Kirby W. Fitzpatrick
Artist
Roger Berry

Architect
Randall Fleming
Artists
Chris Reding
Sam Richardson
Squeak Carnwath
Landscape Architect
Jeffrey Grote

Architects
Future Systems Consultants
  Jan Kaplicky
  David Nixon
Artist
Masayuki Oda

Architects
Arthur Golding and
Associates
Artist
Richard Friedberg

Architect
Ron Goldman
Artist
Lita Albuquerque

Architects
Goldman-Taggart Architects
  John Goldman
  Paulett Long Taggart
Artist
Dan Snyder
Landscape Architect
William F. Peters

Architect
Michael Graves
Artist
Edward Schmidt

Architect
Herb Greene
Artists
J.B. Blunk
Eleanore Bender
Eleanor Rappe
Landscape Architect
Theodore Osmundson

Architects
Grinstein/Daniels, Inc.
  Elyse S. Grinstein
  Jeffrey Daniels
Artist
Richard Serra

Architect
Robert L. Hamilton
Artist
Larry A. Dubbs

Architect
Gary Lee Hansen
Artist
Harriet Johns
Landscape Architects
RSA Land Concepts
  Daniel K. Svenson

Architects
Robert Lamb Hart
Albrecht Pichler
John Petty
Artist
Anna Valentina Murch
Landscape Architects
David Howerton
Anne Haley Howerton

Architect
Henry Herold
Artist
Ernst Neizvestny

Architect
Jonathan Herz
Artist
Jack Scott

Architects
Interactive Resources, Inc.
  Carl H. Bovill
  Thomas K. Butt
  John E. Clinton
  Charles L. Beavers
Artist
Jeffrey Key

Architects
William Jeffries
Associates, Inc.
  William Jeffries
  Jerry Manifold
Artist
William Morehouse
Landscape Architect
Hans Scoffield

Architects
Jennings & Stout
  Jim Jennings
  William Stout
Artist
David Bottini

Architects
Kaplan/McLaughlin/Diaz
  Jeffrey Heller
  David Hobstetter
  John Ellis
  Ellen Harkins
Artist
Beverly Pepper
Landscape Architect
George Hargreaves

Architect
Martin Henry Kaplan
Artists
Gertrude Pacific
Ed Carpenter
Koryn Rohlstad

Architects
Keith, Hall and Bartley
  John Andrews Hall
  Scott Phillips Bartley
  Martin Lloyd Price
Artist
Bob Nugent

Architects
Kemp and Kemp
  Jack Kemp
  Jim Kemp
Artist
Ellen Gunn
Landscape Architect
George Hargreaves

Architects
Jerry Allen Kler
Charles Ashman
Artist
Richard Kamler

Architects
Lawry Coker DeSilva
Architects
  Joel DeSilva
  M. George Lawry
Artist
Carroll Barnes

Architect
James A. Lester
Artists
Karen Carbone
Paul Horsbie
Larry McKee
Landscape Architect
Joe Percival

Architects
Lewis and Associates
  John Lewis
  David Homer Tritt
Artists
Toby Cowan
Max Hein
Landscape Architects
Bob Welborn
Zora Welborn

Architects
Lyndon/Buchanan
Associates
  Marvin Buchanan
  Donlyn Lyndon
Artist
Alice Wingwall
Landscape Architect
Garrett Eckbo

Architects
Meyer, Scherer, and
Rockcastle, Ltd.
  Garth Rockcastle
  Jeffrey Sherer
Artist
Andrew Leicester

Architects
Mighetto and Youngmeister,
Architects and Planners
  Andrew Youngmeister
  Andrew Sinclair
  Mike Hull
  von Roenn Design Studio
Artist
Maureen McGuire
Landscape Architects
Carducci/Herman
Associates, Inc.

Architect
James Monday
Artist
David Lance Goines

Architects
Charles W. Moore
Lisa R. Findley
Artists
Edward C. Moses
Daniel L. Collins

Architects
Stuart Jay Morgan
Dan Phipps
Artist
Jeffrey Owen Brosk

Architects
Neeley/Lofrano, Inc.
 Dennis J. Neeley
 Terryl M. Lofrano
Artist
William Speigelhalter
Landscape Architects
Robert La Rocca and
Associates

Architect
Michael O'Brien
Artist
Valerie Reichert
Landscape Architect
Richard Julin

Architects
Olsen Walker Architects
 James W.P. Olsen
 John Savo
Artist
James Hirshfield

Architects
Pegasus Architecture and
Design
 Jeffrey D. Shorn
 Charles S. Kaminski
Artists
Rhoda Le Blanc Lopez
Gerald L. Thiebolt

Architects
Peters, Clayberg and
Caulfield Architects
 Richard C. Peters
 Richard M. Clayberg
 Thomas J. Caulfield
Artist
Nancy Genn
Landscape Architect
Richard A. Vignolo

Architects
Charles Pfister Associates
 Richard Brayton
Artist
Nance O'Banion
Landscape Architects
POD, Inc.
 Roger McErlane
 Cathy Denio Blake

Architects
Pike/Gentry Associates
 Jerry L. Pike
 James V. Gentry
 William H. Shepardson
 Michael R. Ott
Artist
Clay Jensen

Architects
Rob Quigley
Tom Grondona
Artist
Laddie John Dill
Landscape Architect
Ron Wigginton/Land Studio

Architect
William Rawn
Artist
Michael Singer
Landscape Architect
Michael R. Van Valkenburgh

Architects
Reay Associates
 Donald P. Reay
 Jack T. Sidener
Artist
Maryly Snow
Landscape Architects
Wallace Roberts and Todd

Architects
Rejwan Architects
 Carmella Rejwan
 Darrell Hawthorne
Artist
Paul Kos
Landscape Architect
Roger Franklin

Architects
Roesling-Nakamura and
Partners
 Ralph J. Roesling
 Kotaro Nakamura
 Chikako Terada
Artist
James Hubbell

Architects
Rothenberg Sawasy Architects
 Mitchell E. Sawasy
 Joe E. Guthrie
 Mark Alan Rothenberg
 Kathleen O'Shaughnessy
Artist
Gary Dwyer
Landscape Architects
Emmet Wemple and Associates
 William G. Millsap
 Paul Matthew

Architects
Stanley Saitowitz
Toby Levy
Artist
Elyn Zimmerman
Landscape Architect
Meachem O'Brien Landscape
Architects
 Pat O'Brien

Architect
Igor Z. Sazevich
Artist
Bruce Fraser West
Landscape Architect
Lawrence D. Underhill

Architect
Richard Schoen
Artist
Michael Hayden
Landscape Architect
Norifumi Hashibe

Architects
Seaview Design Group
 Michael Singer
Artist
Bruce Johnson
Landscape Architect
Pamela Burton

Architects
Shen/Glass Architects
 William R. Glass
 Carol Shen Glass
Artist
Peter Mollica
Landscape Architect
Wendy Tsuji

Architects
Clint Sigler
Payo Micheles
Artist
Jose Artese

Architect
Thomas Gordon Smith
Artist
David Lund

Architects,
Henry Smith-Miller and
Associates
 Henry Smith-Miller
 Sam Anderson
 Laurie Hawkinson
Artist
Rudolph Serra
Landscape Architect
Nancy Owens

Architects
Alan Snapp
Brian Clear
Artist
Louise Lieber
Landscape Architects
James Abell and Associates

Architects
Daniel Solomon
Taller de Arquitectura
 Ricardo Bofill
 Patrick Dillon
Artist
Ed Carpenter
Landscape Architect
Barbara Stauffacher Solomon

Architect
Walter M. Sontheimer
Artist
Robert P. Owings
Landscape Architects
Emery Rogers and Associates

Architects
Stoecker and Northway
Architects, Inc.
 John C. Northway
Artist
Claire Ruth Kahn

Architects
Stone, Marraccini and Patterson
 Clark Davis
 James Ream
Artist
Robert Behrens
Landscape Architects
Royston Hanamoto Alley
and Abey
 Robert Royston
 Barbara Lundberg

Architects
S T U D I O W O R K S
 Robert Mangurian
Artist
James Turrell

Architects
Taber Chaitin Associates
 William Stevens Taber
Artist
Douglas Fenn Wilson
Landscape Architect
Andrea Chaitin Taber

Architects
Tanner and VanDine Architects
 James L. Tanner
 Peter VanDine
Artist
David Ireland
Landscape Architect
Mai Arbegast

Architects
David R. Teeters Architects
 Alice Carey
 Michael Ludwig
Artist
Steven Singer

Architect
William Turnbull, Jr.
Artist
Douglas Hollis
Landscape Architect
Edgar Haag

Architects
Valley Architects
 Thomas Faherty
 William Bylund
Artist
Jacques Overhoff
Landscape Architect
Liesle Eisle

Architect
Wilbur L. Weber
Artist
Alan Shepp

Architects
Bruce Weinstein
Ken Saylor
Michael Tolleson
Artists
Randall Lavendar
John Frame

Architects
Widgery-Silk Architects
 Stuart Silk
 Carolyn Widgery
 Geordie Selkirk
Artist
Thomas Lindsay

Architects
Williams and Paddon Architects
and Planners, Inc.
 Jack Paddon
 James Williams
 Jaimi Baer
Artist
William Allan

Architects
Tod Williams and Associates
 Tod Williams
 Billie Tsien
 Robert McAnulty
Artist
Barbara Kruger
Landscape Architect
A.E. Bye

Architects
Willis and Associates, Inc.
 Beverly A. Willis
Artist
Ulisse Pagliari
Landscape Architects
Patricia Johanson
Mai Arbegast